FIND YOUR JOY ZONE

FIND YOUR JOY ZONE

how to see what makes you happy and love what makes you real

anne nelson

SAPPHIRE PUBLISHERS
SIOUX FALLS, SD

Find Your Joy Zone

www.YourJoyZone.com

Library of Congress Control Numbers: 2005911059
ISBN: 0-9773844-3-8

Cover Design by Kathi Dunn, Dunn + Associates, Inc.
Book Design by Liz Tufte, Folio Bookworks
Author Photo by Monica Fehrs

Sapphire Publishers
www.SapphirePublishers.com
Sioux Falls, SD

Printed in the United States of America

Pine Hill Press
4000 W. 57th St.
Sioux Falls SD 57106

Praise for
FIND YOUR JOY ZONE

"Anne's solutions make so much sense for how we live and, more importantly, how we'd like to live."

~ Pat Pearson, MSSW
National Speaker and Author of
You Deserve the Best and
Passion: Rekindling the Fire in Your Heart

"This is exactly what women are looking for and can't wait any longer to find. Anne and her message are irresistible!"

~ Linda Clemons
National Radio Talk Show Host, Author, and Speaker
www.BargainDiva.com

"Anne Nelson's advice for living in joy is not only a formula for a happy, fulfilling life; it is essential to creating a life of abundance. Thank you, Anne, for making it so simple!"

~ Rosemary Redmond
President
Weekenders USA, Inc.

"In all stages of their lives, careers, parenting, relationships, friendships, and more, Anne's book is pointing the way to help women understand their path to success is happy, fulfilling and extremely rewarding."

~ Gale Bates
Contributing Author of *Build It Big*

"Anne Nelson brings women a wonderfully practical approach to making our lives match who we are and what we want most for ourselves."

~ Carol Gruetzmacher
Regional Sales Manager
Big Yellow Box by Crayola

Dedication

To Mom with love, for laying the foundation of living a life in the Joy Zone.

This book is also dedicated to every woman who gets up each day and makes the world a better place, by living in her Joy Zone or striving to get there.

Contents

Acknowledgments 1

Introduction 5

❶ Your Joy Zone 9

❷ The Genesis of Joy 15

❸ Joy Builders 27

❹ Joy Crushers 51

❺ Joy Busters 63

❻ Deliberate Joy 81

❼ Sustain Your Joy 91

❽ Last Words: Generate Your Joy 111

101 Joy-Building Activities 115

Reading Suggestions & Resources for Your Joy Development 119

About the Author 123

A Personal Invitation 125

Acknowledgments

No endeavor is a success on its own. It does take a team and I was blessed from the beginning with a fabulous one.

My partner for life, *David*, thank you for recognizing my need to expand my horizons, encouraging the effort, and, in many respects, putting your own activities on hold. You took on many "extras" so this venture would progress. My children, *Karin*, *Ellen*, and *James*, for providing so many joyous moments in life just by existing in the world as you do. Every time you asked, "How many pages have you completed today?" I knew you understood the bigger picture of what we could do with this book. I appreciate the support and love from all of you, along with the examples of joy you each exhibit day in and day out.

Without the talent of *Susan Kendrick* of Write to Your Market, Inc., the words that express my deepest desires to help others experience joy would never have combined on the pages as they do in this book. Susan, you are a wizard with words. You are amazing, a real Joy Sparkler in my life. *Graham Van Dixhorn*, for reading over our shoulders and adding your insight. You are great at transferring joy right over the phone, too.

Kathi Dunn with Dunn & Associates Design, you truly work magic when it comes to cover design, logo creation, and developing a brand. Your creativity is unmatched and I am grateful that our paths have crossed in this life. *Ron "Hobie" Hobart*'s wisdom and coaching as I embarked on this journey was a like a guiding star. I appreciate your fun energy.

There is a reason and purpose for everything and I am grateful I was introduced to *Kathy K. Grow*, proofreader and editor. You are one terrific woman, with a real ability to connect with others. Your keen eye and knowledge made a difference in the little and final details of this book.

Special gratitude to my fellow writers and editing friends, *Gale Bates, Lisa Tiensvold, and Clare VanBrandwijk*, for your reviews of my manuscript. Your extra eyes, perspective, reassurance, and ideas were just what I needed and I appreciate you. Your friendship is a blessing and your support throughout this journey was divine.

To my mother, *Jane Wick*, for taking my kids so I could write, and for sharing your enthusiasm and inspiration throughout my lifetime. I love you.

To my whole family, *Hal and Jane Wick, Paula, Betsey, and Ross, Wes and Gail Nelson, and all the rest*, I love you all. I am fortunate to have an extended family of support and love for life.

Grandma Dorothy Rance for sharing your cookie recipe. You're the best, Grandma!

Julie Mickelberg, for caring enough to act on my behalf for publicity while on bed rest! Wow. I enjoy our conversations and the memories we continue to create today.

To *my family and friends who have crossed over into perpetual joy*, thank you for keeping the light on.

Jan Tillotson, my business coach, life coach, and friend, for insight, encouragement, support, resources, and helping me stay on target with all my life endeavors. You are an awesome cheerleader.

Dee Van Driel, my personal assistant and friend, for helping me keep my businesses in line and putting perspective on the big picture. I couldn't do it all without your help.

To *Susan Metz, Kyle Greenfield, Kelly Gellerman, Michelle Thie, Julie Mickelberg, Joan Hurley, Janelle Peery, Julie Nielson, Jenny Puumala, Mary Phillipe, Teri Rogers, and all the rest of my tennis buddies* who endured for a year my chatter about this book, who asked often when would it be done and how much is left. I needed that from you and I am glad you were there to ask, encourage, and laugh.

Finally, to all the Joy Sparklers in my life, including *Jan and Mike Naborowski, Rosemary and Rob Redmond, Julie Mucha, Michele Rausch, Joyce Rhone, Diana Swier, and my Weekenders, USA extended family*. You inspire me. *Bob Bailey and George Raynault*, I appreciate the *WOW* factor you have added to life, and I am indebted to the wonders and possibilities of the Universe, and yes, even of myself, that you have made so clear.

My Joy Zone has indeed been expanded through the process of writing this book. My life is truly filled with so many wonderful people that it is both elevating and daunting to name you all, knowing there will be someone's name I have missed. Please know, as a part of my life, you are part of my Joy Zone.

Introduction

Choosing joy in life empowers you and opens you to all that is created for you. It allows you to live in complete freedom, happiness, and joy. Choosing joy in life puts you in control of your reactions to life. And, let's face it, why wouldn't you want joy?

There will be ideas in this book to which you will easily gravitate. There will be some that may make you question me, or yourself. For life to move forward, we need to open our minds, our hearts, and make the choice to take action. I expect you'll discover that choosing joy is easier than you think.

Every day, miracles are happening around you. Every day, you have the power to join forces with your Inner Being, your Creator, your God, to co-create, inspire, and recognize those miracles. Every day, you have the ability to experience joy. "God" as a word has different meanings for everyone. Depending upon the faith in which you grew up, it can mean "Creator," "Almighty," "Father," "Supreme Being," and more—the list goes on. For some it means the spiritual being within oneself, or the Center of the Universe. The concept of "God" is real and comforting to some, but not to others. When I use the term "God" or "Inner Being," please relate to it according to your own belief system.

I have been greatly reluctant to share the woes of my life with others. I always have been one to assess a situation, make choices to carry me through it, and look for ways to overcome any sadness, anger, fear, or loss from the situation. I learned to find a way to reach joy despite my circumstances, and to let go of negative situations.

This tendency to keep my personal life private has enabled me to move forward and to grow my life in the direction I want it to go. I believe, however, there is a price to pay for this privacy, for being a "pillar of strength."

One drawback is that you risk being seen by others as non-social, unapproachable, or even arrogant. Your life may appear "too perfect." Others even may say, "You don't know what it's like . . . you've never walked in my shoes . . . you don't understand."

Another drawback is that you may begin to feel isolated and, therefore, overwhelmed by all the parts of your life you are so carefully balancing by yourself. Ultimately, you pay the price of shortchanging yourself of the joy you could experience by sharing those emotional loads and helping others share theirs.

This isn't about forming a "bleeding hearts" club, focusing entirely on what your troubles are and reliving them every time you talk with others. That only robs you of joy because you can't move beyond your troubles to see what else is there for you. You also risk alienating those around you. This is about sharing yourself honestly in order to create deeper, more meaningful relationships that contribute their own kind of joy to your life, and the lives of those to whom you are closest.

Sometimes it's not easy to find the joy or to choose simply to move on. But it can be done. I've done it and now share with you what I've learned—how I've made the leap to choosing joy—so that you, too, can take what works for you and apply it to your life, easily and effortlessly.

You were meant to live in joy. Those who tell you that to live, you must suffer first, are struggling themselves. Why would God, who created you in His own likeness, want you to suffer? Why would the source of divine being want anything less than a life of joy for you? When you live without joy, you miss the miracles of life; you miss out on the people who have been sent for you to learn from, to enjoy, and to help as well. When you choose joy, you are connected and whole, in alignment with your Inner Being, your God, your Center of the Universe.

A story that awakened me to the realization that there is so much for us to enjoy right now, in this lifetime, describes a woman entering the gates of heaven with St. Peter at her side:

St. Peter walked beside the woman into the grandeur of heaven. They passed a glorious door that piqued her interest. She asked St. Peter, "What's in that room?"

"I don't think you want to go there at this point," responded St. Peter.

But the woman persisted. "No, I want to know everything, now that I'm here."

So St. Peter opened the grand gold doors. Inside were infinite shelves laden with beautifully wrapped packages.

"St. Peter, who are all these gifts for, and what's inside them?" she asked.

"Oh my child, inside these packages are all the gifts God has had waiting for you and all humanity. If you had only asked, they all would have been granted."

I set out to write this book because I believe that joy in life is a choice. We are all entitled, deserving, and destined to a life filled with joy, if we believe it and choose it. What I have come to understand is that many people—maybe you!—need to know there is hope for a life of joy, gratitude, and abundance.

Again, choosing to live life with joy creates power in you. Everything in life becomes easier, more fun, and more free. Discover for yourself the miracles that are waiting for you.

If you want to live with joy, in spite of all that you encounter, then keep reading. Together we will make the journey to creating your Joy Zone.

I choose joy, and I hope you will, too.

1

Your Joy Zone

...We have the tendency to obscure the forest of simple joys
with the trees of problem.
~ Christine Collange

Do you live in a state of "I'll be happy when . . . ," or are you happy in the moment? Do you compromise your personal joy now for the sake of others, with the promise that you'll take care of yourself later?

To live a life filled with joy, you first need to know where you are, emotionally, spiritually, and even physically. Evaluation and assessment are important. This doesn't mean reliving bad memories; this is about reaching inside yourself to honestly look at and see where you are right now.

Joy seems to me to be a step beyond happiness—
happiness is a sort of atmosphere you can live in sometimes when you're lucky.
Joy is a light that fills you with hope and faith and love.
~ Adela Rogers St. Johns

It would be wonderful if you were already in a state of joy. If you are, keep it up and spread it around! If you are not, it's time to make a plan of action!

First, assess your current situation—your home, job, relationships, health, and finances. To choose joy in life, you must assess the choices you have been making and evaluate what your return on those choices has been.

What is it you love about where you are living? Note everything. even if it's simply the view from your bedroom window, or the way the trees shade your yard, how close you are to work, that your neighbors are friendly and the paper boy is a nice kid.

neighbors
close to grocery, clothing and
hardware stores
easy to get to work

Is this enough? yes

What more do you want from where you live? ______________

____

____

____

When you see what you want elsewhere, what is your response?

A. _X_ "They must have paid a fortune to live there."
B. _X_ "I'd have to win the lottery before I could live like that."
C. ____ "One day I'll live there, too."
D. ____ "What am I thinking? I'll never live like that."

What is it you love about your job? Note everything. Do you have good friends there, are the benefits decent, is it an easy drive from home? Or perhaps you're learning skills for your next job—the one you really want!

friends
benefit
line. balance to know more
easy drive from home

Is this enough? ___yes___

What more do you want from your job?

more recognation

respect

____

____

When you see a job or position you want elsewhere, what is your response?

A. _____ "You probably need an inside connection to get that job."

B. _____ "I would have to go back to school to get that job, and I don't have the money or time for that."

C. __X__ "One day, I'll have that job."

D. _____ "What am I thinking? I'll never get a job that great."

What is it you love about your current relationship? Note everything. Is your partner dependable, predictable, caring, supportive, loving, or comfortable?

Caring

loving

Supportive

understanding

Is this enough? ___yes___

What more do you want in a partner or from this relationship?

Supportive

no smoking pot, heavy drinking

____

____

When you see positive, happy relationships, what is your response?

A. ____ "Life is easy for them."
B. ____ "There aren't any good fish left in the sea."
C. ____ "One day, I'll have a relationship that's perfect for me."
D. ____ "What am I thinking? I always attract losers."

What is it you love about your health? List everything, even if it's that clothes are made in your size. Have you felt worse, have you gone a month without a cold, or did you manage not to gain weight over the holidays?

____

____

____

____

Is this enough? ____________________

What more do you want from your health?

____

____

____

____

When you see people around you who are vibrantly healthy, what is your response?

A. ____ "They can eat anything they want and never gain a pound."
B. ____ "It'll take liposuction to make me look like that."
C. ____ "I'm becoming healthier every day."
D. ____ "What am I thinking? I'm destined to be unhealthy and fat."

What is it you love about your financial situation? Are you debt-free, climbing out of debt, able to live month-to-month, able to contribute to charities or retirement funds?

Debt free from credit cards, able to contribute to retirement funds able to put some money into checking

Is this enough? yes

What more do you want from your finances, on a weekly, monthly, or annual basis? to be able to put some more money away for emergency on a traveling spree.

When you see others with more wealth, what is your response?

A. X "Life is easy when you get it all handed to you."
B. ____ "I need a rich man to get me out of the mess I'm in."
C. ____ "One day, I'll be financially free."
D. ____ "What am I thinking? I'd probably just blow the money anyway."

When you can appreciate what others have and enjoy what you desire, when you can appreciate that more really is out there for you, too, and—here's the big one—you can appreciate where you are now, you will be able to make your dreams real. The Universe doesn't say, "Because you are unsatisfied, I'll give you more and more until you become satisfied." What the Universe does say is, "Because you are already satisfied with, and appreciate, what you have, I'll give you more." Your joyful life will attract all that you desire for yourself. You will find yourself in situations that will lead to more of what you desire.

Tally how many *A*, *B*, *C*, and *D* answers you chose above. If you predominately picked *A*s, you recognize that good things in life are there, although it's a huge stretch for you to see yourself having them. A large number of *B* answers means that you want joy and are open to the possibilities, but you see a lot of obstacles. If you chose mostly *C* answers, you have a very positive joy factor, and you know good things are coming your way. If *D*s were the majority of your answers, you've hit bottom and need to be reminded there is hope for a joyful life, no matter what your circumstances. If you're willing to be open to possibilities, this book will bring you much closer to finding your Joy Zone.

Look around. The Universe generally gives back what you give. You have to live in joy where you are, with what you have. What you have in your life—physically, spiritually, emotionally, and materially—is a direct response from God, the Universe, your Inner Being, to how you have responded to what you have and where you are, so far. The reality is, you chose your joy, and you can change it too. Being joyful where you are means having the ability to invite even more joy into your life.

Life events don't happen to you, they happen *for* you. Your joy is determined not so much by *what* happens to you, but by your *response* to what happens. In my life, this certainly doesn't mean there aren't days when I have feelings of frustration, anger, irritation, or sadness. It's just that I prefer the path of joy and all that awaits me there. So, despite any negatives that happen to come into play during the day, I stay on the path and look for moments of joy wherever I can find them. Isn't that the state of being in which you want to live, too?

We come equipped with everything we need to experience
a powerful life full of joy, incredible passion, and profound peace.
The difficult part is giving ourselves the permission to live it.
~ Deborah Rosado Shaw

2

The Genesis of Joy

A child's life is like a piece of paper
on which every person leaves a mark.
~ Chinese Proverb

From your soul to your senses, joy is accepted, rejected, noticed, ignored, savored, severed, shared, withheld, increased, denied, multiplied. You choose when and how to have joy in life. Your choice was influenced by the beliefs that are deep in your soul, planted in childhood, and affirmed through the use of your senses and emotions as you became an adult.

What you believe is what you see—until you learn differently.

Think about how you grew up. Think about your home life, schooling, religious beliefs, friendships. In all areas, well-intentioned people told you what they believed to be true. They all did what they could as parents and mentors to influence you, protect you, and teach you what they thought best for you.

Did you hear statements such as:

- Money doesn't grow on trees.
- Being rich doesn't make you happy.
- We each have a cross to bear.
- Beware the hand of God.
- Children should be seen and not heard.
- Stop daydreaming—you're wasting time.
- With grades like that, you'll never amount to much.

- It's better to give than to receive.
- You can't do that.
- It can't be done.
- It's a hard-knock life.
- Don't rock the boat.
- Don't go against the grain.
- Only in your dreams.
- Only the good die young.
- Life isn't a fairy tale.
- Boys like him are nothing but trouble.
- We all have to pay our dues.
- It's always darkest before the dawn.
- It's a weight you'll have to bear.
- There's a price to pay for happiness.

What other statements did you grow up with in your home, church, and school?

____

____

____

____

Such ideas and beliefs are so ingrained in your thinking, you may not even be aware of them. Still, they impact you and your choices every day. Now is the time to start choosing which beliefs to discard and which truly serve you well. Think seriously about these now because one of these beliefs could be the factor which is preventing you from finding joy in your daily life.

Perhaps you grew up with the popular mantra, "It is better to give than to receive." Because of this, as an adult, you have a difficult time accepting the generosity of others. I grew up hearing, "Bad things happen in threes." For a long time, when something happened to me that I felt was a "bad thing," I expected two more "bad" events to follow.

My internal belief set it up to be my reality. I no longer believe this, so now when one thing happens that I don't like, or that I could label as "bad," I don't automatically experience two more negative events.

Again, many of the beliefs we live by are hard to identify because they are so deeply personal. Others are more obvious because they have become obsolete and we have grown beyond them as a culture. As women of the new millennium, we have discarded many of the ideas—the silent mantras—our mothers or grandmothers lived by. For example, few of us today would agree to live a life based on these beliefs:

- A woman's place is in the home.
- If a woman is to work, it is only acceptable for her to become a nurse or a teacher.
- It's a man's world.
- It's not ladylike to wear pants.
- It takes a good woman to make a man. (Okay—maybe that's one we may still claim—depending on what's in it for us!)

Read any of the many 1950s books on "How to Be the Best Wife," and you'll both laugh and be appalled at the concepts. And yet, those were the beliefs by which a generation lived. Most were simply different from what we choose to live by today. How many of us would wait at the front door at five o'clock, in a pretty dress and high heels, with a newspaper in one hand and our husband's favorite drink in the other, to welcome him home from work to put his feet up and wait for us to serve dinner? Many "how-to" books once suggested that this scenario was just what it took to make a strong marriage and maintain a happy home.

We all get to choose our beliefs. Because of each woman who decided to change her belief from a rejection of working outside the home and the notion that career opportunities for women were limited, to a belief that anyone can pursue the career of his or her choice, we now have many doors of opportunity open to us. And those open doors have led us to run our own businesses, enter the medical or engineering fields, become teachers, or, if we prefer, stay home. Following our heart to what brings us joy is now an acceptable option.

Think back again to those childhood mantras. Ask yourself if they are still relevant to living a joy-filled life. Take the concept of daydreaming, for example. Do you catch yourself now and then in a daydream and tell yourself, "Get back to work; there's not time for daydreaming right now," or "Who am I kidding? It'll never happen anyway?" Is there a Bible verse upon which you're hung up that perhaps was taken out of context? Do you still hear a not-so-favorite teacher's voice in your head, reminding you that, unless you get it right, you'll never amount to much?

Joy Replacement Therapy

You *can* decide to change the negative beliefs you knowingly or unknowingly carry with you. You *can* unload those ideas that hold you back from accepting joy and abundance in your life. Joy Replacement Therapy™ is the way you jump-start your joy from a clean slate. This technique helps you change worn-out thoughts or beliefs, one at a time. Move past an old belief by replacing it with a new one. Consider the new mantras below, or create your own, to replace ones that are not working for you anymore.

Money doesn't grow on trees.	❑ Money grows in my IRA.
Beware the hand of God.	❑ God's gifts of mercy and grace await us.
Children should be seen and not heard.	❑ Children should be seen and heard.
Stop daydreaming—you're wasting time.	❑ Daydreaming is a good use of time.
You can't do that.	❑ You can do anything.
Don't go against the grain.	❑ Be your own person.
It can't be done.	❑ Anything is possible.
It's always darkest before the dawn.	❑ This too shall pass.
There's a price to pay for happiness.	❑ Abundance is your birthright.

Put Joy Replacement Therapy to work for you right now. What other thoughts or beliefs would you change? Write the worn-out belief and then a fresh, new version.

Old:	New:
______________________	______________________
______________________	______________________
______________________	______________________
______________________	______________________
______________________	______________________
______________________	______________________
______________________	______________________
______________________	______________________
______________________	______________________
______________________	______________________

I am learning that if I just go on accepting
the framework for life that others have given me,
if I fail to make my own choices,
the reason for my life will be missing.
I will be unable to recognize that which I have the power to change.
~ Liv Ullmann

When your beliefs are what *you* want to believe, then you'll begin to create your own thoughts, feelings, and behaviors to generate more joy in your life.

Albert Ellis, Ph.D., is widely recognized as one of the most influential psychologists of all time. He is the originator of Rational Emotive Behavior Therapy (REBT) and author of seventy-seven books, including the best-selling *A Guide to Rational Living*. Ellis confirms that we not only create our own feelings, but we usually choose to think and feel in self-harming ways.

According to Ellis, "Just as your thoughts create feelings and behaviors, the latter also affect your thinking. Thoughts, feelings, and behaviors interact with and circularly affect each other." The concept is that your thoughts create your feelings and behaviors. My interpretation is, when you challenge or eliminate negative thoughts, your negative feelings and behaviors diminish as well. In other words, you can *choose* joy.

To take it a step further, what you focus on in life, you get back in multiples, and what you focus on directly affects the flow of joy into your life each day. When you focus on some thought or some feeling that negatively affects you in some way, you need to *replace that thought or feeling.* If you are looking straight ahead, you see one thing; if you turn around, you see something different. The picture changes. In the same way, you need to pivot in your mind from the thoughts or feelings that close off joy to those thoughts or feelings that bring joy into focus for you. Joy Replacement Therapy will help you turn a joyless perspective or situation into one of joyful abundance.

When driving around town one day, I noticed a mother walking with her little boy, about four years old. They were chatting and smiling, but the mother was smoking a cigarette as they walked and talked. My thought was, "That poor boy has to inhale that stuff!"

My value system for smoking is one of "no tolerance." I find it difficult to rationalize anyone willingly choosing to put such toxins in her body, let alone subjecting a child to secondhand smoke. I know that smoking is an addiction that is very hard to break. I also know there are ways to help people who want to stop smoking. I don't view people who smoke as bad people; I struggle with their choice to smoke.

What happened here? On what did I choose to focus? I focused first on that cigarette, which created an instant negative judgment, creating even more negative feelings and emotions.

Time to catch myself, be aware of what I'm doing, and use Joy Replacement Therapy to focus on the joy of this moment. I can have my own beliefs and preferences, but I don't need to let them overwhelm a situation or my emotions so I am left only with negative, judgmental thoughts. There is joy all around us, if we see it. And when we see it, we live it.

I did catch myself. I made a conscious choice to focus on the big grin on the boy's face as he walked with his mother, and on the fact that the mother was spending time with her son. When I shifted my attention from the negative to positive, the positives quickly multiplied. You generate joy in your life by *seeing* the joy in life. It then naturally multiplies over and over again.

Joy Replacement Therapy is one quick way to shift your focus to joy. It's like a bubble bath for your soul. It simply feels good.

Joy Receptors

Joy Receptors are how you put your body, mind, and spirit into a working whole to receive, develop, recognize, feel, and create joy. As discussed earlier in this chapter, you developed certain beliefs as a child that are part of your internal being. In addition, you developed the use of your five senses—touch, taste, smell, sight, and sound—part of your physical being. Perhaps you also developed your sixth sense—gut feeling, inner guidance, intuition, or whatever you choose to call it; this is your spiritual being.

All six senses act as Joy Receptors in your daily life. Think about each sense for a moment. Each has the power to move you past a negative to a positive. Each is a means of getting you to joy instantly. A gorgeous evening sky, the silence and solitude of nature, the sound of robins at the start of spring, or the softness of an old quilt on a chilly day—all can be ways your senses help you experience pieces of joy.

When I walk into my Grandma's house and smell sugar cookies baking, ummm, my mouth starts watering and the joy in my heart is instant. That scent makes me feel good that my grandma is *my grandma*. I appreciate who she is, and that she bakes her famous cookies out of love for us. To hear the oven buzzer go off is like the sound of music to my ears because I know what's coming next . . . more cookies! The sight of six batches of sugar cookies lined up on her kitchen counter makes me smile. The cookies are crisp and crumbly, coated with sugar, and they fall apart in my mouth as I taste their buttery sweetness. Oh my, how they leave me wanting one more, and then just one more . . .

My physical Joy Receptors are working together when it comes to Grandma's cookies!

Are you wondering how the sixth sense, your spiritual receptor, fits in? Consider all the serendipitous moments in your life. Have you ever had a feeling you were going to be the winner in a drawing, and then your name was called? How about when something is missing, but you have that certainty and inner peace it will show up, and then, a few days later, it does?

One stormy summer night at the lake, the kids checked the dog kennel where our golden retrievers play together. Our pup, Penny, was missing. My husband panicked and immediately took off down the road to find her. The kids wondered if Penny would hear him hollering with the waves thrashing against the shore, the wind whipping the flags against their poles, and the leaves rustling wildly in the trees. Nature was creating a lot of noise. I had a gut feeling that Penny didn't run down the road; but rather she was somewhere out by the lake. I followed my instinct and headed toward the lake, in the opposite direction from David. As I rounded the corner of the cabin, from out of the darkness, Penny raced right to me.

In the same way, you can use your Joy Receptors to take you in a new direction when you are feeling stuck or lost. Use them to refocus when unwanted, and unwarranted, childhood beliefs start creeping back into your thoughts. When you fine-tune your Joy Receptors, you are able to perceive even the thinnest vapors of joy—sometimes all there is in certain situations. Develop your Joy Receptors by becoming more aware of them as your guide to more positive life experiences. You will continue to grow in joy.

A realtor who wants to sell your home will encourage you to appeal to the sensory needs of a buyer. Make the house look good by cleaning out the clutter, or make the house smell good by baking a batch of cookies or burning a scented candle. If your senses can help you sell your home, they can certainly help you experience the deeper and more lasting joys in life.

Take a few minutes to consider your senses right now. Don't skip ahead! You'll feel good when you respond to each of the Joy Receptors below.

When I see clear blue skies, I feel peaceful. When I watch beautiful fall leaves turning shades of scarlet for days on end, I feel warm inside. What sights do you recall which enable you to feel good?

____

____

____

____

It makes me smile to hear the playful laughter of children on a playground or geese honking as they fly south. What sounds do you tune into, that bring you joy?

___

___

___

___

I'm grateful that my sense of smell is refined enough to recognize the scent of chocolate, but not strong enough to detect a skunk on the road. A delicious-smelling pot roast in the oven, with all the fixings, provides a sense of security—an "I'm home" feeling. The aroma of fresh-baked bread reminds me of trips to the bakery with my children. What odors make joy well up in you?

___

___

___

___

What tastes stand out for you? Does just thinking about savoring some homemade chicken noodle soup make you feel better inside? Note what flavors make your mouth water and bring you a sense of joy.

___

___

___

___

___

___

Whether it's the feeling you get when your fingers touch a piano keyboard or the keyboard of your computer, there are many tactile ways we experience joy. From the luxurious feel of a cashmere turtleneck to the sweetness of cuddling a newborn, our tactile joys are all around us. I use the same kind of cotton blanket on my bed as I did when I was growing up because it feels comforting when I crawl into bed and tuck myself in. In what ways do you use your sense of touch to bring joy to yourself?

By learning to contact, listen to, and act on our intuition,
we can directly connect to the higher power of the universe
and allow it to become our guiding force.
~ Shakti Gawain

When I ignore a gut feeling or intuition about something, I am generally bothered by what results. When I trust my inner guidance, all goes well. There have been many decisions I've made over the years by relying on my inner guidance, and I've experienced joy in many ways because of that. When have you had a gut feeling or intuition that you followed, and were glad you did?

On which Joy Receptor are you most dependent: touch, taste, smell, sight, sound, or intuition? ______________________________

____

Which Joy Receptors do you hope to fine-tune?

____

____

____

____

Now that you've explored the ways you use your senses, don't you feel good? You've got your Joy Receptors all revved up and you're ready to move on.

To enhance your ability to develop your Joy Receptors even more, I have a gift for you. With permission from Grandma Dorothy, I am sharing her famous cookie recipe (see next page). Make a batch, spread some joy to others, and then enjoy a few cookies as you read the next chapters and discover more strategic ways to build joy into your life.

White Sugar Cookies

from the kitchen of Grandma Dorothy Rance

1 C. sugar
1 C. powdered sugar
2 sticks margarine (not butter)
1 C. vegetable oil

Beat well until fluffy.
Add two eggs one at a time; beat well each time.
Blend in 1 tsp. vanilla extract and 1 tsp. almond extract.

Add:
4 C. + 4 tbsp. flour
1 tsp. salt
1 tsp. cream of tartar
1 tsp. baking soda

Mix well. Dough will be soft.
Chill overnight.
Roll in balls and then roll in sugar;
flatten with the bottom of a juice glass.

Bake at 350° until light brown.

For best results, use an old, well-used, thin cookie sheet—the kind you find in a Grandma's cupboard—and remember to mix in a ton of love.

3

Joy Builders

Joy is the feeling of grinning on the inside.
~ Dr. Melba Colgrove

Each of us chooses our emotions. My ten-year-old daughter Ellen gets angry with me when I say this because, as she puts it, "It's just not always easy, Mom, to change the way you feel!" She's right. *It isn't always easy*. But it *is* within your capacity to do so. No one else determines how you should or will feel. No one can make you feel anything unless you allow it. Sorrow, anger, or fear—all are opportunities to move you to a new level of appreciation, forgiveness, and growth. Ellen is starting to get it. Even at age ten she says, "I know it's my choice, Mom, but how do I do that?"

This is a great question, one which leads us to the steps we can take to choosing joy in life.

A quick way to shift your focus to joy is by using Joy Replacement Therapy and the Joy Receptors covered in Chapter Two. The following 12 Joy Builders will help you practice Replacement Therapy and refine your Joy Receptors. A combination of thought-provoking ideas and action plans, they are designed to help you cultivate joy in your life.

Choose just a few to start. Then, as the process becomes easier, add a few more. You'll develop a pattern for creating your joy in life.

1. Smile

Smiling is the simplest thing you can do, yet it sends a powerful message you feel throughout your body.

The muscle movement triggers the brain to believe it is happy, and it takes fewer muscles to smile than it does to frown. It is widely believed that smiling can lower your blood pressure, relieve stress, relax your body, boost your immune system, and increase your tolerance of pain. Smiling makes you feel better; it really does. So try it!

2. Honor Yourself

My mother is a woman who finds the best in every situation. She doesn't get all wrapped up in negatives; she simply accepts what is, as it is, and moves on. My friends always gravitated to her in high school, and still do today. Twenty years later, my younger brother's friends now gravitate to her. She was then, and continues to be now, an example of living with and choosing joy in life. I applaud the way she reached age fifty and said, "This is when life starts," and then gave me some great advice. Mom said, "You have to learn now to take care of you first. If you spend all your life making sure everyone else is happy, you'll lose yourself. Make yourself happy and, in doing so, you'll be able to help others."

There are so many "how-to" books devoted to creating balance in life. The spirit of these books is in the right place and, for some people, creating a balanced life seems possible. I have kept time studies of my days to see where I'm spending my time. In doing so, I've learned a lot about me. My discovery for my life is that I am not at a point where balance is possible, and understanding this allows me to feel comfortable without balance. One year I analyzed how many hours I had worked, volunteered, spent with family, and dated my husband. I discovered I had spent more than three hundred hours volunteering, just at school, compared to having only four actual dates with my husband. I was giving myself away. Balance is a state of being that only you can determine. You can choose what part of yourself you give to others, and what part you give to yourself.

When balance isn't possible, what there *can* be is joy in the activity you are focused on at present. To devote yourself equally to family, career, and volunteering, and still take care of you, is not always possible.

There are times when one area of life simply requires more of you. There will be times when you give more of yourself, and times when you come first. What others think you "should" be doing is not important. What is important is what *you* believe you should be doing.

Other people will always have expectations of you—what you should be doing and how much time you should be spending on which activities. When you encounter what others think you should be doing, stop, then ask yourself, "Who is this about, really?" Often, you'll discover that it is really about someone else and what he or she wants or believes, and you do not have to own those beliefs, or accept their expectations as relevant to you.

What are areas in which you feel others expect you to participate, but in which, deep down, you would rather not?

miss work because some else ask me to stay home becuz they have a problem. I need to take of myself

In what areas of your life would you like to spend more time?

be with family
be with my friends

Is there an area in your life in which you love to give of yourself, where it feels good to be making a contribution, yet you know it has a negative effect in another area of your life?

by helping people who continue to go on with their problems and not helping their selves

Who do you know who is filled with joy? Who makes you smile, or who is always upbeat about life? List their names below, and what quality about them you most admire.

Randy - makes me laugh,
Smile, caring and loving

Note a time when each was a shining example of joy for you.

when I am told I am
beautiful and a strong person

Why do this? I know your inclination is to keep reading and see what's next. However, it serves you well to do these exercises because, when you start recognizing how others choose joy, the same reality becomes much more tangible for you. See and recognize joy in others and you will find it for yourself, both in the high times and in the low times. What's more, you will reflect joy to others and draw others to you by becoming an example of joy to them.

3. Be Nice to Yourself!

I know how easy it is to beat up on yourself mentally. It's one thing to have high expectations for yourself; it's another thing entirely when your expectations are so high you couldn't possibly reach them or maintain them for long. You need to see the good in what you have right now. Focus on what you do well. Learn to accept that your best is enough. There is too much to do in life to get hung up on perfectionism and unending "I should haves."

Should-haves solve nothing.
It's the next thing to happen that needs thinking about.
~ Alexandra Ripley

The next step is seeing joy for yourself, and this is where using a gratitude journal can help. (Joy Builder #10) A gratitude journal is a terrific reference to which to return and read for a positive perspective on your life. It is easier to berate yourself about what you should have done, but "shoulding" on yourself gets you misery, not joy. Be good to yourself. You are good enough the way you are. Fussing continuously demeans the wonderful essence of who you are.

Create personal affirmations and write them on pretty paper, or use a fun font on your computer; then tape them up where you can see and review them often. You develop a sense of acceptance of who you are, so you can be good to yourself and enjoy all that is around you. I keep two personal affirmations inside the medicine cabinet in my bathroom that I see every time I brush my teeth. I keep two more on top of my desk. They help me stay focused on the big picture and not get hung-up on perfectionism.

Personal affirmations can be about you, your well-being, finances, family, health, or anything that makes you feel good. What the mind sees repeatedly, it begins to process and accept. Here are some examples of affirmations:

- I feel good about who I am.
- I appreciate the abundance in my life.
- My body is healthy.
- I appreciate that I feel good, look good, and enjoy all that is around me.
- My family is physically healthy, financially fit, and spiritually sound.
- I am spiritually connected to my Source, and experience joy in my everyday living.
- My best effort is enough in all that I do.
- I appreciate the miracles I experience every day.
- I am a winner.

- I am a growing, spiritual being, living with joy every day.
- My life is filled with fun and laughter.

About what do you want to feel better?

take care of my health
able to help other people
(when I can)

Write two affirmations that fit this need.

healthy body

When you treat yourself well, others will, too. You deserve to experience joy in all you do. Choose two affirmations that feel good to you and post them where you'll see them often—the refrigerator, your work environment, or even in your laundry room, so you see them every time you throw in or fold a new load of laundry.

There are only two ways to live your life.
One is as though nothing is a miracle.
The other is as though everything is a miracle.
~ Albert Einstein

4. Look for Miracles

Notice the miracles around you, and joy will be present. Notice the budding of a flower, a purring cat, your dog's loyalty, unexpected income, a friend's phone call, a child finally getting that "aha!" in math, or your kids playing together all afternoon without fighting. There are miracles around us all the time. Then there are those miracles when your intuition steps in. Perhaps, you choose a new route to work, then discover later it helped you avoid an accident. You truly do see—and find—what you look for.

I once lost my wedding ring and didn't want to tell my husband. I often take it off when I am exercising, playing tennis, or typing at the computer. After several days, I found the ring in my office, deep in the carpet next to my desk. The miracle was a divine nudge that prompted me to look again, just one more time, so I would find the ring before the vacuum cleaner sucked it up.

What small miracles have happened in your life in the last week?

____

____

____

____

When Ellen was seven-months-old, I placed her in a walker, the old-fashioned kind with four wheels, no locking brakes, and a tray in front to hold toys.

Ellen loved being in her walker because she could bounce around and stand up. She had never managed to move it forward or backward by herself, however; she was quite stationary. One day I moved her walker outside the bedroom where I was cleaning for a few seconds, but, in those few seconds, she figured out how to put one foot in front of the other and proceeded to tumble down the six steps to the living room. In horror I tried to catch her, but she had momentum. Guilt gripped me as terror raced through my mind; my child could be severely injured, and it would be my fault.

When I reached Ellen, she was crying and scared, but otherwise okay. Amazingly, she wasn't hurt at all. I know divine intervention broke her fall, and I am grateful that she wasn't injured. (I often wonder if that incident was the beginning of today's daredevil ways!)

What are some of the bigger miracles you've experienced?

Still being alive after car

accidents

Another time, I was standing in the kitchen, talking on the phone, watching my three-year-old son outside on the swing set. He was in his own world and completely happy, swinging as high as he could. Then, as if everything turned to slow motion, I saw him fly out of the swing and soar at least eight feet in the air. I threw down the phone and ran outside. I couldn't get there fast enough. James had landed flat on his back, and I was certain we'd be headed for the ER. But, by the time I reached him, he was already up. I was totally shocked. In my mind, there was no way he should have been able to get up and walk around, and yet he didn't have a bruise, cut or scratch. This is how miracles happen for us, right before our eyes, even though, in the midst of our panic, we don't always see them at first.

How about your own near misses, like car accidents that could have been deadly, or at least damaging? From the dangers of water sports and snow sports, to harsh weather experiences, there are miracles every day in our lives. Recognizing these miracles when they happen gives you reassurance that the Universe, or God, is working in your favor, and life as you know it is okay. This is the very root of joy.

List a few times when miracles happened for you or your family, or for your friends.

Surviving car Accidents
Sister still surving from
cancer

When you look back on these times, aren't you filled with a sense of inner peace and gratefulness? This is when you start to smile and find there *is* joy in your life.

Give your problems to God. He's going to be up all night anyway.
~ Anonymous

5. Meditate or Pray

With any challenge or frustration, remember to take it to God, or the Universe, in prayer. You have the Divine Source and the assistance of the Universe holding you up at all times, and responding to your desire for joy. When you waste energy and shut off your connection to your Source, you can summon assistance back into your life.

Modern medicine now sees the value of a partnership with religion and faith. More than half of the country's medical schools offer spiritual medical care courses as part of the curriculum. Harold G. Koenig, M.D., a leading authority on religion and medicine, is the author of sixteen books on the subject, including *The Healing Power of Faith—How Belief and Prayer Can Help You Triumph Over Disease*. Many studies validate the positive power of prayer in contributing to improved health. Larry Dossey, M.D., an internal medicine practitioner and executive editor of *Explore: The Journal of Science and Healing*, experienced many patients finding their way to better health because of their spirituality, their belief in a higher being, and their religion. He studied the role of spirituality in health and went on to write nine books, including *Prayer is Good Medicine*. Today there is scientific evidence that prayer can have a compelling effect in healing our illnesses.

I have a deck of angel cards to which I refer daily. They always make me feel connected to the wonders of God's presence. It is absolutely uncanny how often I will ask a question, say a prayer, then flip a card, and God's angels are right there, speaking to me, offering me hope, assurance, peace, and the direction for the day I really need. When I've hit a low point or a point of uncertainty, talking to the angels always provides the road back to joy. You may find that saying a rosary, meditating, reading scripture, or another form of focus may be just what you need. Try different approaches.

The important thing here is to speak to your soul and listen for the answers.

6. Defuse Tension

When tension builds up, you may find that your entire body tightens. Tell yourself to relax your shoulders, to stop wringing your hands or tapping your feet. Instead, keep your hands and feet busy in a positive way. Work in your garden, play the piano, clean a closet, or bake cookies. Exercise or yoga is great way to defuse tension built up in your body and mind. Or simply take a nap if you need one. Find an outlet that helps you let go of tension. One friend of mine goes all out, cleaning whatever she can, when she is overloaded with tension. She made my kitchen sink sparkle one day. When she was finished, she was a new woman . . . and my sink looked great!

What are the best ways you defuse your tension?

driving around

read

go for a walk

7. Tackling the "To-Do" List

There can be such pressure to achieve in life, to be the woman who can do it all, from volunteering, to having a career, to raising a family and dealing with all the dynamics that go with that. Trying to keep up with it all can diminish our joy from day to day.

Even in the midst of working on this book, I found myself once again having to review my own schedule and expectations of how thin to spread myself. For everything to which you say Yes, and add to your calendar, there is something else to which you are saying No. I was saying No to sleep and eating properly. I was also shortchanging other areas of my life that bring me joy. Some of us need to remember we can't do it all, nor should we try. Sometimes it is better to let others do it and give them the credit, so you are able to enjoy other areas of your life more thoroughly. Joy is diminished when you overload and fail to appreciate what you are doing. Joy is enhanced when you give yourself the freedom to make choices that are right for you.

List the times you overloaded your schedule today, this week, or this month.

____

____

____

____

How did you feel at the end of the day, week, or month, in which your schedule was overloaded?

____

____

____

____

An extensive list of "to dos" can quickly overwhelm and shortchange you. You will miss the joy of completing all those tasks to the best of your ability. I am a list maker and often get wrapped up in a list a whole page long, one which still doesn't even include typical daily routines or things I really *want* to do. I know I have a lot I need to accomplish each day. I find, however, that the more "to dos" I must shift from one day to another, the more anxious I feel. And when I am tense, anxious, and frustrated, I see and feel less of the joy around me.

An idea which has made a great impact on me is writing two lists—one for me, and one for the Universe to do for me.

First, I divide a sheet of paper into two columns. On the left side, I list what I must do that I know I can commit to completing that day. A rule of thumb is to list the six most important items and prioritize them. Beyond those six are items I want to get done, but, if not done today, I'll still live. On the right side, I list everything I want to get done, but, the reality is, without more than twenty-four hours in a day, it will be impossible. This is the list I want the Universe to take care of for me. Then I focus on the list on the left side—"my list"—crossing off items as I go. I mentally let go of the list on the right side and, before I know it, those tasks are being completed by others. People with whom I need to connect call me, saving me the time of calling them. Project details seem to resolve themselves. Details for which I don't have time eventually fall into place, and I am more joyful for it. The stress level of wanting to accomplish so much, or the compulsion to feel like I *should* accomplish so much, is drastically diminished.

This double list also keeps my long-range "to dos" in one spot so I don't forget about them, while keeping them out of my day-to-day planning so they don't overwhelm me. Every month or so, I look at and highlight the items that are completed. I am always amazed how those things get done—or at least get started—maybe because they are not staring me in the face every day. If I want to, I may shift an item from the Universe list to the daily list, if it is in dire need of some immediate attention.

8. Take a Time-Out

A thirty-second time-out will refresh you and help you replace a negative thought. Visualize what makes you happy; watch a little movie in your head. I often see my husband and I sitting in the shade in Jamaica, enjoying the warmth, the peace, and the freedom from the responsibilities of our everyday lives. Or I picture myself wrapped up in a warm blanket on the couch, reading a good book and drinking hot chocolate. Olympic athletes are often coached to visualize themselves performing at their personal bests in competition, seeing themselves on the victory stand, because the mind believes what it sees. The mind sees in pictures.

Where could you go right now in your mind that would be a good "time-out" for you? Be sure to make a detailed picture in your mind.

____

____

____

____

Finding joy in everyday life, even in areas that frustrate you, happens when you create solutions to your overflowing daily agenda. When you are in a tizzy, and life is not going as you please, you can shift gears. Take thirty seconds to shift your focus. Close your eyes, breathe deeply, and remind yourself that whatever challenge you have at the moment, "This too shall pass." Turn on your favorite music and dance, or belt out a tune.

Schedule an extended time-out for yourself. Take a friend to lunch and catch up on your relationship. Take a hot bubble bath and light a soothing, fragrant candle. Allow yourself to have some time at a spa for a massage or body wrap; do something that will soothe your senses and open your mind and body to joy. Run, walk, rock climb, pet your cat or dog. If you don't start taking care of you, who will? Whether you take a thirty-second, thirty-minute, or three-hour time-out, the point is to take care of you, so you are able to shift your focus and realign yourself for experiencing and choosing joy.

9. Elevate Others

Elevator calls are ones you make to someone else to share a funny story, give appreciation, or spread joy in other ways. Do your friends live far away? Buy a long-distance phone card or use those free weekend and evening minutes on your cell phone to make some elevator calls. When you make elevator calls, you are uplifted, too.

My long-time friend Michelle lives out-of-town, and we don't talk often. She called recently and we talked for an hour. It was such fun to catch up, I called her back the next week, and we picked up our conversation where we had left off. It was wonderful to laugh together again, share stories, give advice, and support each other. She is a joy in my life, and just writing about our phone calls makes me happy.

Who are the friends or family with whom you want to reconnect? These are not obligation calls. Obligation calls do not bring feelings of joy; they only complete a duty. Make the fun calls. List the friends and family you want to call, and check them off as you do.

__________________________ __________________________

Let your heart be awakened
to the transforming power of gratefulness.
~ Sarah Ban Breathnach

10. Write in a Gratitude Journal

First find a beautiful journal, one with plenty of blank pages, or use an already-dated daily journal, whichever you prefer. Each night before bed, take a couple of minutes to list five things for which you are grateful that day. Sometimes your list will extend beyond five gratitudes. Sometimes you will find you were only grateful that you had a frozen dinner handy to heat in the microwave or that no bills came, that you had a good hair day, no cavities when you went to the dentist, or that tomorrow is Saturday. The more habitual you become about keeping a daily gratitude journal, the more peace and joy you will find in your life. It will become a subtle yet powerful presence.

Other people will see it, too. Sometimes they will even tell you that you seem happier, calmer. Maybe they will say you are acting like "you" again. One day on the tennis court, after I missed an easy volley I should have aced, costing my teammate and me the game, my opponent commented to me, "Normally you'd have gotten pretty upset. I can't believe how calm you are today." I was having fun and felt good about myself that day. I had an inner feeling of joy. Several bad shots later and I still felt it, and she noticed, smiling as she shook her head. I can't say every game since then has left me feeling like that, but that sense of inner joy and calm is becoming more frequent—the new norm.

Consider your *usual* bedtime routine. Do you go to bed thinking about the news you just watched? I don't watch the evening news before bed because it is generally depressing and negative. I have not yet found a news channel all about what is right in the world, that reports the great things teenagers are doing today, the positive examples corporate executives show in their businesses, or the happy and life-giving marriages in the community. These wonderful news events are happening, but they don't sell like the bad stuff. So, until they do, I'll focus on my own gratitudes before bed. Doing so helps me sleep better, wake up rested, and set a tone of well-being for the next day.

Two psychologists—Dr. Michael McCollough of Southern Methodist University, Dallas, Texas, and Dr. Robert Emmons of the University of California at Davis—conducted a research project, involving several hundred people and their experiences of gratitude and thanksgiving. The results of their study matched my personal results in many ways. Those individuals who regularly experienced gratitude and thanksgiving reported feeling optimistic, enthusiastic, energetic, and loved. Gratitude is attracting the interest of researchers, Web sites, and books, and, for those who make thankfulness a daily practice, is resulting in joyful living.

My gratitudes range from how appreciative I am that the day was beautiful to how happy I am my children have good friends, from appreciation for the spouse I have to the friends and family in our life. I get very specific. I am grateful for:

- walking four miles with my friend Kristi.
- the way my daughters play so well with their cousins.
- getting the broken sink replaced.
- a safe trip home.
- the relationship and marriages our parents have.
- fun neighborhood children.
- moments that remind me why I love my kids.
- taking a nap today.
- time for myself.
- a really great haircut.
- the first snowfall of the season.

Your gratitudes will be whatever comes to mind, whatever you feel thankful for. Some days they will be big and some days they will be small. Everything has value when it enables you to have joy.

Here's a side note for you. I am even grateful when my husband snores! For years I viewed it as a total annoyance. However, when I started to see it as a reflection of his ability to relax, to find his total realm of peace and tranquility, I could live with it and actually appreciate it. It's like listening to a giant lion purr, and this reminds me he is a wonderful man. He is the strength his patients need in life, he is the solid rock of our family, and he is my chosen partner in life. Though I don't wish to fall asleep to it every night, I no longer feel anger and frustration when he starts in with his nightly symphony. Remember, you get what you focus on, so when I choose to stop focusing on the frustration of his snoring, it becomes less an irritation.

Reflect on your present blessings,
of which every man has many;
not on your past misfortunes,
of which all men have some.
~ Charles Dickens

When you focus on the frustrations in life, you get more of them. Sometimes a situation will actually worsen, or other areas will also begin to fall apart. The more you focus on the ugliness or injustice in the world, or in your life, the more often you see it. When you start to recognize the goodness all around you, that multiplies. When you choose the joyful side of life, you experience more of it.

On one occasion I was at a business dinner discussing the challenges of the sales field at the time. I overheard one of my colleagues tell another woman that she needed to try the approach I was taking. I had shared with her that I was keeping a gratitude journal, that I was not focusing on what was *not* working, but rather on what *was* working and on how to help the field improve. My colleague had been lamenting that her sales force was not happy. They were frustrated with the economy and tired of the company's challenges. She was wondering what would come next. I didn't see things as desolately as she did, nor would I chime in and reinforce her negativity. The concept of focusing on that of what you want more, by recognizing the greatness in everyday living through a gratitude journal, began to impact her. By starting her own gratitude journal, she was able to alter her attitude, gain personal strength, and positively impact the attitude of her sales force as well.

There is no instant fix in life. Life is a process, sometimes one that needs to be revved up each morning when you awake. Choosing to live a life filled with joy is a process that requires a shift in your thinking and actions. Keeping a gratitude journal can help move that process along.

You don't just jump from frustration to joy. It's a process, a step-by-step, one-thought-at-a-time process.

When something does not insist on being noticed,
when we aren't grabbed by the collar or struck on the skull by a presence
or an event, we take for granted the very things that most deserve our gratitude.
~ Cynthia Ozick

11. Read Uplifting Books

The concept of "garbage in, garbage out" is accurate. What you put into your mind is reflected in how you live! That is a revelation that came to me through years of reading and of observing others. When you revel in the negative, you emit negativity, sarcasm, or pessimism by the words you use, the reactions you have, and the actions you take. If you find you are troubled by grief, frustrated by an unhappy relationship, or challenged with financial woes, books and professionals in those specific fields can help you get past these obstacles and create a positive shift. When you replace a negative feeling with a positive feeling, you begin to rise to a state of understanding and peace, and you bring joy back into your life.

How do you carve out time to read, given your responsibilities at work and home and all that you have on your "to do" list? Well, you've found time to get this far in this book! The methods you used to find time to read this may be just what you need to use to read more. Carve out fifteen minutes to read when you get up in the morning, listen to books on tape when you're in your car, or start a book club. A book club, in addition to providing the benefit of reading more often, also gives you a social outlet with people you enjoy. Imagine how grand a day can be when you start with a positive feeling. If you are not a morning person, spend fifteen minutes before going to bed, or in the car while waiting for the kids after school, reading an uplifting book. Keep a book with you for those unexpected times when you have to wait for an appointment or get stuck in traffic. There will always be time for the things in life that are most important to you.

Does TV consume your time? It's so easy to get sucked into an hour or two of watching television, especially if you are really tired and one of your favorite movies is on. The body and mind shut down, and you temporarily become a zombie, clutching the remote. If you really love a certain movie, videotape it or buy the DVD. Most hour-long TV programs are actually only 38 minutes; the rest is eaten up by commercials. You will carve out 20 minutes to read if you cut out the commercials.

Consider, for a moment, the commercials to which you are subjected. Pharmaceutical companies will quickly have you believing you have some ailment or disease that requires a visit to the doctor. Their drug is the cure you need in order to feel better. In your repeated concentration on the symptoms of the disease, you may very well manifest it. This is "garbage in, garbage out" in the worst way. Be in control of what you put in your mind. A good book will yield more joy, with "good feelings in, good feelings out."

In your journal, list the books you read each month. Being able to look back on your year and see the number of books you have read will do wonders for your morale. I feel a sense of accomplishment when I see how many books I manage to read during a twelve-month period. Keep a list in the back of your journal of the books you want to read. I always keep a list in my personal digital assistant of books I want to read so, if I ever catch myself traveling or in a bookstore and can't think of a book I have not read or want to read, I'm set.

Reading a good book is a powerful way to discover resources for finding and creating joy, and also for simply shifting your thoughts, for the moment, to a positive perspective.

What books do you want to read but have not yet read?

___

___

___

12. Create a Book of Memories

You know those funny stories about your kids that make you laugh until you cry, the pranks a coworker pulls that leave the entire office in tears from laughter, or the happy times you have with friends and family? Write these down in a memory book. A memory book differs from a scrapbook because it is all written, not a combination of pictures and journaling. When it comes to memories, the details can fade if you don't write them down promptly. It only takes a couple of minutes to jot down the incidents and dialogue you want to remember.

Include those little snippets from life that make you laugh, or things your kids say that make you smile. When our son James was four, we took him to a basketball game at the Catholic high school in which, as a fundraiser, the seniors played against a team of priests. James saw our parish priest come in and said, "Look, Mom, God's here!" In Ellen's second-grade classroom, a visiting seminarian was talking about wildlife and showing slides. Ellen had only one question on her mind, so she interrupted the slide show to ask, "How did you know God called you to be a priest?" Six months later, he left the seminary. I still wonder if she had an internal feeling that he really didn't belong in the priesthood, and if her question prompted him to reflect on his vocation. A year later, he was married. When President Reagan died, James caught a glimpse of the funeral service on TV and sadly said, "Oh boy, the government died."

What stories have been told and repeated time and again in your circle of friends, at work, or in your home? Often we forget those stories when a new and funnier one comes up. My children's thoughts, concepts, and perceptions get to my heart every time. A memory book ensures you won't forget. It also makes you feel good and helps you center yourself when you need a boost of joy.

Once, I was attending a week-long training seminar for women, and had to leave my three-month-old daughter at home. Since I was breast-feeding, I took along a breast pump in order to express and be able to continue breast-feeding when I returned home. At lunch, I told my roommate I was going to run up to our room and express, and I would be back before the training started again. Another dear friend was sitting with us and, being completely unfamiliar with the processes of breast-feeding and expressing, asked me, "Is Fed Ex coming every day to take your milk back home?" I had to conceal my disbelief and laughter to respond, "Oh no, I just dump it, but this way my milk doesn't dry up and my breasts don't leak." My roommate must have told the story a dozen times to our colleagues at that training.

Another memory for our whole family took place during early December 2002. David and our oldest daughter, Karin, were away hunting for the weekend. I was at home with our three-year-old son, James, and our other daughter, Ellen, who was nine. Ellen is our dramatic child, so much so that we often don't put a lot of stock into what she tells us.

Early in the evening, Ellen was downstairs practicing piano, James was watching a video, and I was on the main floor, talking on the telephone. Ellen came upstairs and told me there was a man in the basement. I told her I was on the phone and to go practice. She came upstairs again, saying, "MOM, I can hear a man in the basement!" My response was total disbelief: "Ellen, I am on the phone. It'll wait." She refused to go back downstairs. When I got off the phone, I was mad at her for messing around when she was supposed to be practicing her piano. I told her we were going to go downstairs and that I'd show her there was no one in the house but us. James came down with us.

Our stairway is an L-shape, finished underneath for storage. The piano is just on the inside of the "L" against the wall, near the door to the storage room. Our furnace room is situated just behind the stairwell. When we got to the basement, I went over to the storage unit to prove to Ellen there was no one in our home. As I opened the door, I heard a man moan in a soft voice, "Help me!"

Animal instincts to protect one's children really do take over! I screamed at Ellen to get out of the house, grabbed James under my arm like a football, and we all raced upstairs. Ellen ran to the sliding glass doors off the kitchen, and I went right out the front door to the neighbor's house, running and screaming, "There's a man in my house!" I was picturing a man in my furnace room, lying on the ground, pleading for help, in who-knows-what kind of condition.

My neighbor Brad, his son, and a number of college hockey buddies, were standing in Brad's garage. When I came running in, Brad told me to stay there, then said to the guys, "Let's go!" One stayed behind with me as the others raced off in two directions around and into my home. I was a shaking mess when it occurred to me, "This is when I'm supposed to call 911"! I panicked, thinking of the guys' safety in my home, with an intruder there.

In Brad and Shelly's kitchen, I called 911. I was hyperventilating, and Shelly tried to calm me down. The woman on 911 asked questions and told me to stay put, just breathe, and not to hang up until the police arrived. Moments later, five police cars and two fire trucks pulled up with their lights flashing.

I went out to meet the police as Brad and the boys came out of my home, assuring me there was no one there. They had been through every closet in every room, and no one was there. I was adamant to the officer and Brad that I had heard him; I knew he was in my house. Brad assured the police again that there was no one there. The police officer told me we'd all go in and check together. So, three police officers, two firemen in full gear, Brad, and I went into my house and downstairs. One fireman went into the furnace room, and one checked out the storage room. As we opened the door, I heard it again and, boy, did my emotions fly high then! But only *I* heard it. The officers didn't!

Then I heard it again. This time I turned around and looked at the computer in the corner of the room. A "Clifford the Big Red Dog" math game was on the screen, and a man in a balloon, stuck in a tree while trying to get across the river, was saying, "Help me." The volume on the computer was so low it sounded like a whisper, *and* it sounded very real. Well, between having been so afraid and then feeling really foolish at all these police officers, firemen, and Brad coming out for this non-emergency, I freaked out.

I stood in complete shock, apologizing profusely. The officers assured me it was okay, it was their job. One fireman gave a "knowing" nod to his partner, and they all left.

Later, together back in the house, Ellen, James, and I sat on the couch, watching Christmas movies, as I debated whether to call my parents and ask them to come get us for the night. The phone rang. It was my husband David, wanting to tell us about their hunt and ask how our day was. I let Ellen tell him all about it and then got back on the phone. Intellectually, I knew we were okay and there was really no need for David and Karin to come home; emotionally, however, I was a wreck. Two hours later, they were home. Three days later, I was able to go into the basement again.

My mother, finding the whole story quite funny, e-mailed it to everyone in her address book. Mom said it was a good night out for the firemen and police officers as it gave them a good story to laugh about for a long time, and, with a recent spate of house fires in our city, they needed a good laugh.

Not all my memories are this dramatic, but many are uplifting or funny. This one makes me laugh even now. I don't want to forget these times, nor do I want my children to forget. This is where a memory book has great value. Keep it in the kitchen so you can quickly and easily write down your kids' funny comments, or in your desk at work to record the humorous antics of a coworker. Memories that make you laugh until you cry are the kind to enter in your memory book, along with life events that make you smile. When times are rough or your focus just needs a minor shift back to joy, reading a few entries in your memory book can really do the trick.

What are the first three memories you want to record in your memory book?

____

____

____

____

____

Another easy idea for remembering fun events in life came from my friend Barb. She used to keep index cards in a kitchen cupboard. When her children did something extraordinary, funny, or silly, or reached a monumental growth curve, she'd write it down on an index card so she could add it later to their baby books.

For a quick fix to finding your Joy Zone, use Joy Replacement Therapy to shift your thought process to be open to joy. Carve a little time out for you each day to begin increasing your joy. Use one of the twelve ideas here to start taking care of you on a bigger scale. Remember the 12 Joy Builders from which to choose:

- Smile
- Honor Yourself
- Be Nice to Yourself!
- Look for Miracles
- Meditate or Pray
- Defuse Tension
- Tackle the "To Do" List
- Take a Time-Out
- Elevate Others
- Write in a Gratitude Journal
- Read Uplifting Books
- Create a Book of Memories

There are so many ways to create joy in life. The gratitude journal is the most powerful way to start. Smiling is an easy action you can do right now, and all the time. Next, move to the ideas that feel best to you and, as life progresses, add more of these. You'll discover new beliefs about life, living, joy, and how you want to live each day. When you start to use these ideas for creating joy, you will discover a few more of your own. When you do, let me know. I will pass them on. I am always looking for more ways to find joy for myself and to help others do the same.

4

Joy Crushers

The marvelous richness of human experience would lose something of rewarding joy if there were no limitations to overcome. The hilltop hour would not be half so wonderful if there were no dark valleys to traverse.
~ Helen Keller

So let's talk life events—the big ones. I've had them. You've had them. These are the ones that cause you to question the entire scheme of things. These are the ones that generate a huge sense of loss, anger, frustration, and despair. These are the challenges that make you wonder if there will ever be joy in your life again.

When crisis mode hits, you need to go into crisis management, not only to survive, but also to get back to joy in life. Emergency trauma teams are taught to approach each crisis with four basic steps: remain calm, assess the situation, treat the worst first, and evacuate the scene.

When you experience a personal trauma that feels like a crisis, take the **B.O.L.D.** approach to survival, recovery, and joy:

Breathe deeply. (Remain calm.)
Open your eyes. (Assess the situation.)
Look for help. (See what needs attention first.)
Discard pain and depend on divine assistance. (Evacuate the scene.)

In crisis mode, you need to put out your Joy Receptors big time! Remember which Joy Receptor you depend on the most: touch, taste, smell, sight, sound, or intuition. Life's Joy Crushers do not have to be permanent. You can and you will survive, thrive, and live with joy again.

Story #1

Here's a story about an event that put me into the Joy Crusher mode for an extended period of time. In August 2002, I received second-degree burns on my right hand from hot oil that splashed over the edge of a pan while I was cooking. This pain was unlike any I had ever experienced. I could feel the heat of the burn clear down to the bone, even when my hand was submerged in ice water. For two days, I could still feel the intense heat. Twice a day, for six long weeks, the bandages had to come off so my husband David could clean the burn, and rewrap it with fresh bandages. This was followed by several weeks wearing a white cotton glove, to keep my hand protected from the elements during the day and to hold in a burn medication cream at night.

During this experience there were many disappointments. I missed my kids' first day of school, tennis (for three months), a national conference at which a dear friend received an award, and other events I could not attend because I was either in pain or too doped-up on pain medications.

Getting dressed was a major challenge, from head to foot. I could not hook my bra, zip my pants, or tie my shoes. There were so many mundane chores I couldn't do, or couldn't do easily, for weeks and, some, for months. Being right-handed and losing the use of that hand caused a real loss of independence.

At the same time, some incredibly good things happened during that period. The burning oil did *not* hit my then three-year-old son, whom I was holding at the time. During my recovery, my family came to the rescue, as they always do when needed. My mom helped with the kids, getting them to and from school. She got me to doctors' appointments, bought me tank tops with built-in bras, cleaned my house, and helped with chores. My sister-in-law made meals for our family. My mother-in-law helped with errands and more kid chauffeuring. Get-well cards came from many people in my life. The kids' teachers and classmates prayed for me daily. David was especially attentive as he continued to care for and bandage my hand daily. All these experiences enabled me to see and experience joy through those days of recovery.

Another gift during this time was working with an incredible burn specialist. Because of his skill and expertise, I did not need a skin graft, and my hand healed in record time. At each of my appointments, my doctor and I had some wonderful conversations about healing. He was always amazed at how fast my healing was coming along. He couldn't believe how the scars were fading, since scarring is one of the biggest concerns with burns. At my last appointment, he leaned back in his chair, shook his head, and said, "People just don't heal this quickly." Then he paused and added, "Unless they are very spiritually connected." He waited for my response.

I shared with him that, since some of our friends were experiencing health challenges, I had been reading many books about the power and assistance of angels in our lives. I had learned to trust there was a greater power at work in the healing.

At one point early on, when pain medications were unable to provide any relief, I sat down in a chair, laid my hands in my lap, closed my eyes, and called upon angels for divine assistance. In my mind, I pictured bright warm lights surrounding me. I remember my body trembling, my eyes watering as I held back tears in response to the pain. I literally said, "I can't take this; please release this pain." And in minutes, I had relief. I asked for divine assistance for rapid healing, and for when the pain was beyond my tolerance. I believed I would heal without permanent injury or scarring. Each week I took pictures of my hand, and the rapid rate of healing was apparent. I was grateful for my healing progress. The resources for assistance are bigger, and go far beyond, the physical presence of people who aid us in our need.

Medical research compiled over the last decade confirms the power of prayer, laughter, and positive thinking in healing the body. Stories abound of cancer patients who heal despite all "logical" reasons they shouldn't. Type "Mind & Body Research" in an Internet search engine, and you'll come up with thousands of sites linking to this research. Bookstores and libraries now have an array of books devoted to the concept of integrated medicine. Extensive studies continue to explore how thoughts, prayer, and imagery affect the health of people today. One such book—loaded with more than sixty essays, all extensively researched by renowned leaders in scientific, medical, social, and other health-related fields—is *Consciousness & Healing: Integral Approaches to Mind-Body Medicine*, by Marilyn Schlitz and Tina Amorok, with Marc S. Micozzi.

Think back to your own life circumstances. When have you experienced a loss of independence? Perhaps yours was related to an illness or a broken limb.

In looking back, where were there moments of joy for you?

Is there more you need to do to regain independence and experience joy in your life? Do you need to seek counseling? Could physical therapy help? Are you able to see the joyous events and moments wrapped up in your situation? Have you looked for signs of divine intervention? Reflect on these questions for a few minutes and expand your answers beyond a quick "yes" or "no" to include "why."

Taking action to resolve a situation and improve your life is your first step in experiencing joy. Considering the questions in the paragraph above, and your own situation, what steps do you need to take so you can experience that joy?

____

____

____

____

Remember to use the **B.O.L.D.** approach when you are in crisis mode:

Breathe deeply.
Open your eyes.
Look for help.
Discard pain and depend on divine assistance.

You may need to sit in a comfortable chair and literally concentrate on your breathing. You will discover a sense of calm coming over you. Then, actually or mentally, open your eyes and see what around you is good. Look for help in the people around you. Talk to them, appreciate them, and love them. If the situation merits, get professional help so you can talk out that which you need to unload. You may find it a challenge to discard pain, whether physical or emotional; however, ask for—and expect—divine assistance to carry you through, and you will survive with your joy intact. Reread this book to regain your focus on joy. Remember you are not alone; a greater force is out there waiting to help.

Go back to the story at the beginning of this book, in which the woman enters the gates of heaven and sees a room full of gifts. Ask for and expect the gifts you need right now: relief from pain, the right people to come into your life, assistance to get through a Joy Crusher. And, always, expect there to be times of joy despite the Crusher you are under. As you take this approach, you enable your Joy Receptors to be sensitive to what's happening around you. This approach helps bring back joy.

Story #2

Another Joy Crusher many people experience at some point is financial collapse. This is not just month-to-month financial stress. This is deep, watching-the-bottom-drop-out, financial devastation.

This hit me in 2001, when I had a major falling-out with a business partner. We were the closest of friends, masterminds working together in a fun creative business, with broad visions and gigantic dreams. Unfortunately, her personal financial troubles started rolling over into our business, creating a huge difference of opinion about her personal use of money from our mutual business account. She then declared bankruptcy, leaving me with my financial loss, plus hers. This amounted to more than most dual-income American families make in a year, so the loss was significant.

This was a betrayal unlike any other. Where was the joy at the end of each of those days?

I was angry. I felt betrayed. I shed tears. I had fears for our finances. I was ashamed for not seeing it coming. I felt naive. But I also kept my head up enough to see the smallest signs of joy—simple things like a picture my daughter drew of our family with the words "I love you" scrawled on it, my two-year-old son hammering a nail into wood with sheer delight, a phone call from an old friend, and freshly fallen snow glistening in the sunlight.

Financial challenges are huge. They reach beyond your bank accounts, stressing every other area of your life. If you find yourself in a position of financial distress, get help. There are resources, from books and credit card counselors, to tax and financial advisors. Getting the assistance you need will help keep the stress from disabling other parts of your life, and preserve a frame of mind that allows joy to be present. Keeping your spirit fixed on even the smallest joys is what will see you through.

True richness is attained when
our net worth and self-worth
have met the challenges of life
and risen above them.
~ Suze Orman

Big life traumas such as physical limitations or financial challenges do not have to inhibit joy. You can take action and choose to look for joy. Life events can affect your emotional self, tearing at your soul and shattering even your desire for joy. These defining moments can rip your heart out, or, if you choose, be a major opportunity for change and transformation in your life.

Story #3

Going back further, my freshman year in college proved to be one of personal growth because of the ugly experience of date rape early in the school year. I went through denial and the whole range of self-doubts I now know typically characterizes a woman's response to this kind of situation. I wondered how I could have let this happen to me. Had I set myself up for this? Maybe there was some lingo on which I had missed out—I thought "no" meant no. Mentally, I had to accept this was rape, even though it wasn't as brutal as what I'd seen in movies or read about in magazines. I questioned how I could have prevented it, and felt ashamed, angry, and self-conscious whenever I saw my "date" on campus. I struggled with whether or not to tell anyone. In the aftermath, I made poor choices. I skipped classes and partied and drank like crazy, trying to discover who I was and if I was ever going to have a real relationship, or if I even wanted to. I struggled to define myself at a time when everything left me feeling strange and disconnected.

Only my roommate knew what had happened. She was supportive, but the day she told me I had become a "wild woman" and needed to stop, I knew she was right. I had joined a sorority and the sisterhood I experienced was what I needed to discover my own value again. The grade standards were what I needed to get myself back on track. The encouragement from other members helped me recognize my own gifts and talents again. My confidence in who I was started to grow. One ugly incident in my life would not determine who I would become, or keep me from what I dreamed of doing in my life.

At that age, I was not far enough along in my personal growth to be fully aware of, or even able to define, what it meant to choose joy in daily living, although I was beginning to experience it. I didn't think of living with joy as a conscious choice. I did discover, however, that I was in control of my emotions. I was the only one who could determine how I would react and with what feelings I wanted to live. This discovery was a launching pad to my choice to live with joy in my life.

> ...It isn't until you come to a spiritual understanding of who you are
> —not necessarily a religious feeling, but deep down, the spirit within—
> that you begin to take control.
> ~ Oprah Winfrey

When have you struggled with anger, betrayal, financial challenges, or other life issues?

____

____

____

____

____

In looking back, what were the big or small happenings about which you could be happy during your struggles? Remember, it might have been as simple as hearing your favorite song on the radio, seeing a comic that made you laugh out loud, or hearing the laughter of others.

____

____

____

____

____

If you are currently in the midst of challenging life events, open your eyes wide to see what moments of joy there are around you. Maybe the doctor was able to find the source of your illness. Perhaps someone befriended you by shoveling your walkway on a snowy day or sharing a loaf of banana bread. Did a child hold your hand or give you a comforting hug? When you open your eyes wide, what are the moments of joy surrounding you?

____

____

____

____

To whom can you go for help?

____

____

____

____

Are you trying to be superwoman and handle everything on your own? I know how easy it is to take that approach. I'm a superwoman wannabe, too, but I can tell you from a lifetime of personal experience, you *can't* do it all alone and still *survive with your joy intact.* Breathe, get help, and pray for divine assistance.

Divine love always has met and always will meet every human need.
~ Mary Baker Eddy

Now think again. What did you miss? I'm betting there was more. Who has helped you physically, mentally, emotionally, or silently during your struggles?

____

____

____

____

What positive distractions were happening around you?

____

____

____

If you have been victimized or traumatized by a life event and are struggling on your own to live through it, there are good, solid resources to help you. It is not a reflection of inadequacy to seek out psychological help when you need it.

Even after my financial loss, I had to learn to stop reliving things in my mind. Sessions with a certified counselor helped me gain a new perspective when I was unable to get past the anger toward my former business partner, and toward myself.

Story #4

A major step in a woman's life is the decision to have a child. Everything changes when a child arrives—*everything!* Like many couples, my husband and I were excited about the prospect of getting pregnant, and having fun dreaming about how our lives would change.

Our first experience with conception, however, turned out to be devastating. But divine intervention can work in our favor time and time again, and this time was no different.

After doing rounds at the hospital one Saturday morning, David came home —something he never did—before going to work at the Air National Guard. When he came into the house, he found me passed out on the bed. I still had a pulse so, fueled by fear, he scooped me up and drove me to the ER. There must have been angels at every intersection because he drove through several stop signs and a few red lights on the way.

In the ER, an ultrasound revealed that an ectopic pregnancy had ruptured the fallopian tube and caused excessive bleeding. My blood pressure dropped, I went into shock due to internal bleeding, and I was rushed to surgery. Four hours and two transfusions later, I was finally back in the recovery room.

Though our loss was immeasurable, there were positive Joy

Distracters everywhere. A caring and loving ER nurse continued to visit me in the hospital. My family went to great lengths to connect with each other so everyone would know what was happening (not as easy in those days before cell phones). My sorority sisters were all in town and came to my side with their support during this scary time. A friend delivered muffins to cheer me. I received more than six hundred cards from students who wished me well and were anxious for my return. Good things *were* happening in the midst of a sad situation.

Through every step of the event, there were miracles and gratitude, as divine intervention pulled together my family, the doctors, and the generosity of so many others. I don't carry this sadness with me today; I carry a sense of joy for all the miracles and the wonder of what transpired during that time. Although I felt sorrow, loss, anger, and depression, I know that, had I let this overwhelm me, I likely would not have conceived our first-born daughter just four months later.

If you have experienced a devastating event and continue to relive it today—keeping it as an excuse, as guilt, an injustice, or even a sorrow that consumes your thoughts or your prayers—you can overcome it. You may need to take the Look-for-Help step. You are intended to live with joy, not sorrow.

What event in your life do you need to let go? Describe the experience.

____

____

____

____

____

What moments of joy and miracles did you experience at the time?

____

____

____

Recognize the miracles, divine interventions, and joy-filled moments that enable you to discard burdens and to choose to live with joy each day.

Change your focus from the sadness or badness of a life event. Step back, accept it for what it is, and ask for divine assistance to see the light beyond the situation. Walk away, and then be thankful for the joy that will come to you as you keep moving ahead. Enable yourself to see the miracles and feel gratitude in the midst of a Joy Crusher. Remember to follow the **B.O.L.D.** steps:

Breathe deeply.
Open your eyes.
Look for help.
Discard pain and depend on divine assistance.

Life happens every day—good, bad, exciting, painful—all of it happens. The way you choose to respond to the experiences of life determines if it will crush your ability to experience joy or will help you rebuild. I want to encourage you to take the steps to have joy in your life again.

Accept the pain, cherish the joys,
resolve the regrets;
then can come the best of benedictions—
"If I had my life to life over, I'd do it all the same."
~ Joan McIntosh

5

Joy Busters

We may miss a great deal of joy because we expect it to be unusual, dramatic, and spectacular. We are waiting for lights to flash and bells to ring.
But the truth is that joy is here, right now,
waiting for us to notice it.
~ Veronica Ray

Unlike Joy Crushers—the big life events that impact our joy—Joy Busters are those little everyday things which affect our ability to live with joy in the moment. Believe it or not, they are within your control—your complete control. I will admit, though, it isn't always easy! In this chapter, you will discover simple steps for managing the five Joy Busters and increasing your joy in the process.

The five most common Joy Busters are Sleep, Exercise, Nutrition, Finances, and Attitude. It seems easy enough to say, "I will sleep enough, exercise enough, eat well, control my finances, and keep my attitude positive." The reality is, however, any one of these Joy Busters can totally be out of whack, immediately impacting the other areas. Read on now and find how to address each Joy Buster and how to manage that aspect of your life, thus increasing your total joy. It may take patience, and it may take practice, but you *can* do it.

Joy Buster #1: Sleep

While listening to the radio, I heard the disc jockey ask the question, "What do women get one hour less of than men every day?" I immediately called the station, got through with the right answer, and won a free lunch at a new local restaurant. The answer? Sleep!

The first major Joy Buster is lack of sleep. It may feel like you are superwoman when you can "manage" on little sleep, getting up at 6:30 A.M. and finally collapsing into bed again at 1:00 A.M. But, over time, this totally zaps your body. You begin to move in slow motion, except for the times you give your body a jolt of caffeine, or those days when you crash and burn and then take a day off to sleep and reenergize.

I used to chuckle at others who told me they needed eight hours of sleep a night. I usually functioned on five and considered it a badge of honor. I now know that I need seven hours of sleep a night, and to get eight is a real blessing. I really do function much more productively and enjoy my days when I'm not "asleep at the wheel," mentally or physically. Sleep experts say that most adults need seven to nine hours of sleep a night. Are you one of the 47 million adults who do not get sufficient sleep?

Research shows sleep deprivation can have many negative effects. It makes you crabby. Sometimes you don't even see it, but others do, especially your partner, kids, and coworkers. They see it *and* feel it. It also causes poor judgment, lack of productivity, and a breakdown of your immune system Even aging and diabetes are impacted by sleep deprivation, according to the National Sleep Foundation. And all this means, ultimately, that lack of sleep robs you of joy.

Think about your evening routine. When you decide to go to bed, do you walk to your bedroom, brush your teeth, put on your pajamas, and go to bed? I'll bet not! You know the routine. After you announce you are going to bed, you check all the doors, make sure the kids are tucked in, switch loads of laundry, turn on the dishwasher, answer the last few e-mails, shut down the computer, write out your "to do" list for the next day, check the kids' backpacks, write checks for the bills, put away the toys on the stairs, press clothes for the next day, then finally head for bed, hopefully taking a few minutes to wash your face—if you aren't too tired at this point. Whew! What a routine! It's a woman thing.

Men announce they are going to sleep and promptly head off to bed, only taking time to drop their pants on the floor and brush their teeth. Does this sound familiar?

It was not an easy conquest for me to let go of more hours awake to get more time to sleep. Remember, I prided myself on being able to operate on so little. I tried keeping a chart of my sleep times so I could see if I was increasing my sleep. But it didn't work. I tried to shorten my "to do" list but found myself adding on those extra details anyway, because I couldn't rest until I did. I couldn't see the tradeoff in getting more sleep. Then we went on a family vacation, and I finally got it—enough sleep, that is—and the reason for it.

During our vacation, we spent so much time outdoors, swimming, touring, and having fun, that, by 10 P.M., we were exhausted. My husband and I put the kids to bed and—since I was not home to fall into my usual pattern of checking e-mails, running one more load of laundry, finishing the dishes, and doing the bills—we both went straight to bed. Each morning I discovered how good it felt actually to have slept for eight or nine hours. I would eat a good breakfast and then head right back out for another full day of fun activities.

Amazing what getting away from home did to help me appreciate sleep and my ability to finally get it. I had energy to go all day with the kids. I had much more patience. With a sense of calm, I handled experiences which normally would have sent me into a litany of, "What's wrong with these people?" I could think clearly whenever I took time out to write. What a major impact, from such a minor change.

That vacation helped a lot, but it was tough to keep sleep a top priority once I returned home. At least I had experienced all those great benefits and knew what I was working toward. I still don't have the magic cure for getting the sleep I need. Try as I might to create a system for regular sleep so I could teach you the same thing, it just isn't there. The reason has to be within you. When you desire to live each day to the fullest, really to recognize and experience joy, you will find a way to start getting to bed earlier, too. Maybe not every night, but more than before. Believe, me you will respect yourself more in the morning!

The Great Sleep Challenge

How many hours of real sleep do you get a night? ________________
How many do you need? ____________

For one week, challenge yourself to go to bed at a reasonable time. I rejoice every time I make it to bed at a healthy hour. What's reasonable for you? How about thirty minutes or even fifteen minutes earlier than usual? Start small and build. You may need to leave undone a few things around the house, but as your body becomes relieved by the downtime—actual rest—you'll find yourself with the energy to do what needs to be done in less time . . . and earlier. You will expand the task at hand to fit the time you have allowed. Have you ever found you can get the house cleaned in an hour when you know guests are on the way? If you allow yourself the right to go to bed thirty minutes earlier, you will manage to accomplish in the remaining hours of the day the tasks that need to be done.

If you already do well getting the sleep you need, congratulations! You are an inspiration to the rest of us and a sign of hope that it is possible.

There have been times when I have fallen asleep in tears but in my dreams the most charming forms have come to cheer me up and I have risen fresh and joyful.
~-Johann Wolfgang Von Goethe

Joy Buster #2: Exercise

Do you want to ensure that you sleep even better and function with a clear mind each day? Exercise is a huge contributing factor. It's a fact: Exercise reduces stress, which in turn enables you to get through daily routines and tough times with greater ease. If you already exercise regularly, good for you! If you don't, good for you, too, because you now have a starting point for improvement.

Do you have an unused membership at a health club? Do you have a collection of videos and DVDs for reducing your thighs, strengthening your abs, or tightening your buns, all gathering dust? Do you feel like you've tried everything—aerobics, yoga, kickboxing, and circuit training?

After years of trying it all—owning everything from a rowing machine to barbells and steps, and having memberships at various health clubs—I finally stumbled across what works for me. I play tennis three times a week at a club, lift free weights twice a week at home, do sit-ups and floor exercises for fifteen minutes daily, and occasionally walk on the treadmill. Though I do find I get sidetracked when I travel or when the "to do" list becomes too long, I really feel better when I stick to this routine. I have more energy, and my clothes fit better, too. And of course, all this gets the joy flowing.

How's your exercise routine? Do you exercise daily? Once a week? Hardly ever? What routine?

____

What have you tried that didn't work?

____

____

____

____

What have you tried that does work?

____

____

____

____

Describe the ideal exercise routine for you.

____

____

____

What will be your start date? ____________________

Write a commitment statement to yourself, expressing what you intend to do and why you are committed to doing it.

____

____

____

____

How might you sabotage this new routine?

____

____

____

____

Did you skip the last question? I know when you're inspired and full of optimism, it's easy to think nothing will hold you back or get in your way. But old habits die hard. So take just a moment to answer the question above. Knowing in advance what you might possibly do to sabotage your new commitment, puts you in control. You will know exactly what to look out for, what to monitor, and what to strengthen.

Joy Buster #3: Nutrition

Nutrition is also a factor in your ability to live with joy. When your system has the proper nutrition you need, wow—look out!

When I decided to lose weight, I read books and kept track of my food intake and times of eating. I learned about nutrition, proportion, moderation, and balance in eating. Once I began to understand and provide my body with the right amounts of proteins, fruits, vegetables, and dairy I needed daily, I was amazed at the weight I lost.

In addition to losing weight, I began to—you got it—sleep better, too. I was more alert and clear-headed during the day. I had a new and better perspective on what was happening around me. I found the good in situations instead of the horrific—always an option when you are exhausted and feeling sluggish.

But the best part of eating well and being at the weight you want to be is this: *You feel good.* It is so much easier to find joy in life when you know you are healthy and you look and feel your best. Others notice, too. You will find you get comments about how you manage to do so much, questions about why you seem so happy, or compliments about how you're glowing. You'll discover that what you are doing to the inside of your body is also affecting the outside. Your emotional life benefits because taking care of your body creates a sense of stability and calm.

Now remember, you may slip back into old routines. It happens gradually. When it does, regroup and start again.

One morning, feeling groggy and sluggish when I got up, I mentally retraced my actions from the day before, focusing particularly on the foods I had eaten:

cereal
nutrition drink
half a leftover fast-food sandwich
piece of white cake—the corner piece with lots of frosting
triple-thick milk shake—just a small one
frosted cookie
chocolate birthday cake
grilled steak
French fries
strawberries
another frosted cookie—only half this time
margarita

Talk about slipping backward. This was a landslide. What a lousy way to treat my body!

Excessive days like this bog you down. You become lethargic and unaware of the miracles and joy around you. Your attitude shifts to mediocre and complacent rather than upbeat and happy. Whenever you slip up, don't worry. Enjoy the cheat and then start over. Each day is a new day, so each day you have a new opportunity to make it a healthy, well-rested day, *full of joy*. From there you are much more able to make clear choices, and enjoy yourself in the process.

One step that can make a difference in your nutrition intake is to create a weekly or monthly menu. When you see it on paper, you will notice the gaps in the food categories. This will make grocery shopping easier, too. When you have all the right ingredients on hand, you can shift menus when you are not in the mood for what you had planned.

What are your favorite foods in the following categories? You can pick specific ideas from these lists and add more of your own.

Proteins/Main Meal

Lean beef, eggs, venison, fish, soy, and seafood are a few ideas with which to get started.

____

____

____

____

Vegetables

Don't get stuck listing just what comes in a can or from the freezer section of the grocery store; most have too much sugar, sodium, or preservatives in them. Think fresh produce and seasonal vegetables for the best flavor and maximum nutritional content.

____

____

____

____

Fruits

Like vegetables, some fruits are better at different times of the year. Keep in mind, too, some fruits are very high in sugar content. When I have a rushed day, sliced apples are a quick and easy addition to a meal, saving me time while ensuring we get a fresh fruit with dinner.

____

____

____

____

Grains/Pasta/Potatoes

This is not an excuse to carbo-load! But some carbohydrates are good for the body. There are a lot of foods in this category that are healthy, nutritious, and often overlooked. For example, you may want to include sweet potatoes (without the marshmallows and brown sugar), whole grain pastas, wild rice, and brown rice.

____

____

____

____

Desserts

This is not to say you should have dessert with every meal, but it is nice to know what everyone likes when you want to celebrate a special occasion.

____

____

____

____

Before you move on to the next step, go back and add a few no-cook or super-simple-to-prepare items in each category for those days when you are on the go, or just want a break from the kitchen.

Now, put your favorites together to generate a menu for one week.

Sunday:

Monday:

Tuesday:

Wednesday:

Thursday:

____

____

____

____

Friday:

____

____

____

____

Saturday:

____

____

____

____

Are you starting to get the feel of this? Post a calendar on the refrigerator, and fill in a dinner menu for each day. Keep a grocery list right next to it so you are prepared when it's time to shop. We do this in our family, and it has helped to eliminate both the "Do I have to eat that?" syndrome and just giving up and heading out to the first fast-food restaurant upon which everyone agrees.

If you have a family to feed, ask everyone to contribute his or her list of "like it or leave it" foods. Armed with this information, not only is it easier to eat well, it makes it easier to please the multiple dietary demands of a family.

The secret to experiencing joy in life
is loving what you have
while you're working toward what you want.
~ Ruth Ross, Ph.D.

Joy Buster #4: Finances

Number four is such a big issue, it will have a book all its own someday. I don't want you to wait, though, so let's take a hard look at it right now. ***IT*** is the number one strain on marriages today. ***IT*** keeps thousands of young adults living at home with their parents, long after the traditional college years. ***IT*** is the use of money, your financial situation, Joy Buster #4. Money issues can absorb joy faster than you can say, "Charge it." Troubled finances literally suck the joy right out of your life until you are left with nothing but worry, and money issues alone consume your thoughts.

If you are suffering from financial stress, get help. Financial planners, bankers, and/or nonprofit debt consolidation agencies, can all help you get back on track. Start today to look for ways to move beyond your current situation and its pressures.

These commonsense ways can get you started.

1. Know how much money you go through in a month. Think beyond monthly expenses and include annual, biannual, and quarterly expenses as well, such as insurance payments. Financially challenged or not, you will keep more of what you have if you know what you have and what you need.

What is your monthly income? ____________________

What are your monthly expenses? __________________

Which expenses are necessary: clothing, food, rent/house payments, insurance, student loans, etc.?

____

____

____

____

What expenses are incidentals: electronics, gadgets, fast food, entertainment, travel, etc.?

____

____

____

____

What is the last item you bought that you know was a frivolous expenditure?

____

____

Overspending on credit cards
merely to accumulate things to wear or display or to satisfy the desire for traveling,
eating out, or entertainment is
paying tomorrow for today's pleasures.
~ Suze Orman

2. Never spend what you do not have. If bills are flooding your mailbox, or if getting bills bothers you, it is a sign you are spending what you don't have and cannot afford. If you are unable to pay your credit card bill each month, you need to start using cash only, until you learn to spend within your means. One good strategy for changing bad habits is to watch and learn all you can about money from people who have it. Watch your self-talk here, too. Shift from thoughts of "I can't afford it" to "I will purchase it when the dollars are available." Often when you wait to purchase something you desire until you have the cash flow, you discover you really don't need it. Or if you do, and then you get it, it is a much greater joy!

Curb your impulse buying with these three quick tips:

A. Make a list before you go shopping, and if what you want to put in the cart is not on the list, don't buy it. Chances are high you'll forget about it by the time you get home.

B. When you put something in your cart that is not on your list, take it out. When you get to the checkout line and still believe you really need it at that point, go back and get it. Often, you will discover your cart is already as full as you want it, or you are out of shopping time.

C. Do not remove tags until you are ready to use the item, and clip your receipt to the item. If you don't wear it, use it, or play with it, within two weeks—take it back. You do not need it. And, with the receipt handy, you have no excuse not to take it back.

3. Start now, if you have not already, to set money aside as an emergency fund. Six months of income invested, but readily available in case of need, is a smart backup plan. If six months feels overwhelming to begin with, set a goal for three months and then build from there. It

may sound impossible to save that much, but you can. Start small, be consistent, and do not compromise your commitment.

4. Decide how much you need to enjoy the lifestyle you want. Learn from others who have done it. Develop a plan to get to that point. *Stick to it.* You deserve it.

What does the "ultimate lifestyle" look like to you?

____

____

____

____

What are the first three things you will do to start yourself on the path to reaching the lifestyle you desire?

____

____

____

____

What is the driving force for you to do the work necessary to make your financial plans happen?

____

____

____

____

5. Give to others. It feels good to be able to make a difference in the lives of others. The amount is not what is important; the simple fact you care enough is what is important. Even the wealthiest of the

wealthy will tell you they always get something back in return for what they give. *They get back good feelings*. It feels good to benefit others who need the help. Want to really experience a deep feeling of joy in your heart? Give to a charity or someone who is in need, and watch the benefits spread because of your generosity.

When have you been on the receiving end of a financial windfall or even a small assistance that made a difference in your life?

____

____

____

____

When have you given to others in need and experienced the pleasure of someone using your gift?

____

____

____

____

What is your ultimate goal for giving this year?

____

____

____

____

Thoughts are energy, and you can
make your world or break your world
by your thinking.
~ Susan L. Taylor

Joy Buster #5: Attitude

Does your attitude tend to sink or soar? A negative, sinking attitude will block joy. Anger, resentment, grudges, and sarcasm, work like plaque in the artery to the heart. You can't see it, but one day it clogs up and the result is a heart attack. The heart may be a muscle that pumps blood through your body, but it is also the emotional center of your life.

Scientific and medical researchers are finding a strong correlation between an unhealthy heart and negative attitudes and stress. When traumatic stress hits, stress hormones are released that actually can cause elevated blood pressure. This puts strain on your heart and puts you at risk for a stroke. In the book *Consciousness & Healing: Integral Approaches to Mind-Body Medicine*, renowned cardiologist Dean Ornish writes, "We have to deal with the emotional heart, the psychosocial heart, and the spiritual heart." The heart is not just a mechanical device, a muscle in the body. It is the epicenter of our deepest emotions.

Taking small steps toward joy—focusing on little leaps toward joy versus gigantic issues surrounding a bad situation—will help diminish anger and soften the blow of negativity on an experience of joy.

Think about your attitude. Do you generally see the cup as half full or half empty? Do you use the words "at least" more than the words "there's only"? Do you say, "At least we found a parking space," or, "I can't believe there's only one parking space left"? Again, letting go of grudges, anger, resentment, and sarcasm, and shifting to acceptance, forgiveness, and appreciation, will make a tremendous impact on your ability to find and experience joy because your heart will be open to it.

Your attitude in life is a reflection of your soul. Create an attitude which generates and encompasses joy. Consider where you are, and make a conscious decision to grow and maintain a positive attitude.

Check the following Joy Busters you have already mastered in your life. Then number the remaining Joy Busters in order of which ones you want to focus next on improving.

____ Joy Buster #1 Sleep

____ Joy Buster #2 Exercise

____ Joy Buster #3 Nutrition

____ Joy Buster #4 Finances

____ Joy Buster #5 Attitude

What is the first step you will take to break your priority Joy Buster?

____

____

____

____

What will be your next step?

____

____

____

____

When you are thinking joy,
you are emanating joy all around you.
~ Ruth Ross, Ph.D.

This is a big challenge, but *you are ready* for it! Try, over the next fourteen days, to see how a new, healthier, Joy Busting habit in your lifestyle opens more avenues for joy. It takes twenty-one days of repetition to create a new habit. Go for a full month and experience the profound pleasures of pure joy.

6

Deliberate Joy

Never regret. If it's good, it's wonderful.
If it's bad, it's experience.
~ Victoria Holt

If you live with deliberate joy, you reach the point where your life is full, but full of what *you* want. Living with deliberate joy gives you the ability to experience life around you on your terms. It is having good things in life flow to you. It is living guilt-free and feeling satisfied and confident about the choices you make. It is letting go of obligation, and acting from an innate point of desire. It is a new level of self-discovery that brings you back to the point of being able to dream again, to recognize the miracles around you. Living with deliberate joy fills your soul with the warmth and love of all that is intended for you by your Creator.

It has been my observation that, for the most part, men are good at taking care of themselves. They don't question if they should go hunting, fishing, golfing, or to a car show, or watch Monday Night Football religiously. We could learn a lot from them. It is not wrong to take time out for yourself. That is what rejuvenates your soul, mind, and body. Taking those time-outs, both big and small, is all part of living with deliberate joy.

Every summer, my father-in-law reminds us that the time he has spent at our family's lake cabin over the past thirty-five years has brought him peace. It is a place to simply relax and feel good. When a reunion of his extended family came around every year, his contribution was to print and mail out the invitations. Then he skipped the event. He said, "Why, out of obligation, would I give up a weekend, when I would rather be at the lake spending time with my immediate family?"

I used to think, "What a selfish thought. You should want to build those relationships. It's just one weekend out of every year, right?"

He has it right for his life, though. He does not sacrifice taking care of himself for the sake of pleasing others he doesn't even know well. And he is happier for it.

There are times you may feel obligated to show up at events or alter your schedule to accommodate someone else's activities: Fourth of July parties, holiday gatherings and concerts, weddings and christenings, and more. When you receive an invitation, first be honored you were asked, and then hold back your RSVP until you know for sure you want to attend. When you decide you are going because you *want* to go, you will enjoy the event.

When have you put what others thought was a necessary obligation ahead of your priorities, and then regretted it?

____

____

____

____

____

What did you give up that you would have enjoyed doing?

____

____

____

____

____

If you could go back in time, how might you have handled this situation differently?

____

____

____

____

If a similar situation arises again, how will you handle it?

____

____

____

____

When I was a teenager, I could tell my mom had unhappy times because she was always taking care of others first. She put everyone else's "to do" list before her own and constantly volunteered to help others with their projects or needs. Everyone loved her because they could depend on her. When she began putting her own needs first, however, she became happier. She still helps others, but has learned to ask herself, "Will this disrupt my own needs?" She began to live with deliberate joy.

Think for a moment about *living with deliberate joy.* Remember my mother's advice? "You must take care of yourself, because if you don't, you won't be able to help anyone else." You cannot make others happy, only yourself. And if you are not happy, it is a challenge to fully give of yourself to others. When you take care of you, you are living deliberately, with intention, and this puts you in your Joy Zone.

It is only in your thriving
that you have anything to offer anyone.
~ Abraham-Hicks

Once the full force of motherhood hit me, with kids going in every direction—homework, activities, car pools—I fell into the trap of believing it was my responsibility to cater to everyone else's needs, to ensure their happiness. In the process, I somehow quit taking care of me. I had forgotten the advice Mom had given me.

I began to question what I was teaching my daughters as well. Was I unintentionally teaching them to sacrifice their own needs and desires in order to accommodate the desires of others? Why would they ever desire to be a grownup—a wife or a parent—if they believed it meant giving up oneself entirely to do it? I wanted to teach my girls that their desires are valid and important, and it is okay to pursue them.

It's all very subtle. Children are influenced by so many factors. I want my influence to be positive and to provide a foundation of joy. I made up my mind, my children would grow up with appreciation for what they have, and would respect that being a member of a family means we all get to enjoy life, but not at the expense of anyone else. Often I will say to my kids, "Friday is your day. You can have friends over, and I'll take you where you need to go. Then, Saturday is my day." They have learned the world does not revolve around their personal needs *all* the time. They recognize that we all have needs. Our household is much happier now, because I took control of ensuring I get the time I need, too. In essence, my family lives with the fair compromise that each of us is entitled to live with joy, but not at the price of another family member's right also to live with joy.

When have you felt that everyone else's needs came before yours?

____

____

____

____

____

____

Whose needs tend to take the most out of you, and how do they manage, unintentionally or otherwise, to shift the focus to their needs at the expense of yours?

____

____

____

____

____

How could you change the situation so everyone can have time for himself or herself without you sacrificing your needs?

____

____

____

____

____

When situations come up which could alter plans you've just made, how will you manage that? For example, your favorite organization, ____________________ (insert name), needs a chairperson for the annual ________________ (insert event), and—since you have done it the last four years—there is just no one who can take your place. After all, your talents benefit so many! They "can't do it without you!" How do you see yourself maintaining your integrity and your deliberate joy in this situation?

____

____

____

____

I found myself in this position with an organization for which I often volunteered. I loved being part of it. It felt good to know I was making a difference in the lives of those in need. But, at the same time, I desperately wanted time to do my own things. Every time I thought, "I'll take time to write tonight" or "I'll finally get those half-finished projects done," I would get a call from a member of the organization with an "urgent need," and I would relinquish my personal time to meet the needs of others. My writing, personal projects, and hobbies were constantly taking a back seat, and my frustration level was increasing. The Joy Zone in my life was waning. I could hear my mother's wise advice reminding, "Take care of you first."

Then I remembered the tattered sign in the registrar's office at the university: "An emergency on *your* part does *not* constitute an emergency on our part!" I had to summon the boldness to say, "I'm sorry, I have other commitments." Those commitments were to me! I had to complete my own "to do" list, write, play with the kids, go to lunch with a girlfriend, visit Grandma, get caught up with the laundry, run all the little errands on my list—and I deserved the time to do it. And the more I did it, the more satisfied I became with me. My joy was back on the rise and life is better that way.

You deserve to take care of you. You don't have to make excuses. Simply say, "I'd love to help, but I already have commitments." Practice saying this. Say it out loud right now. Go ahead, try it. It's not hard after you've said it a few times. The joy comes back. I'll bet you can feel it already.

When you take control of taking care of you, then, when you do help others, you do it out of desire, not obligation. When you help others after you have taken care of you, you do so with joy.

As I watch my mother care for my grandmother, I see it as a labor of love on my mother's part. She wholeheartedly wants to do this. I do not see frustration in her about this situation. When she needs a break, she enlists the help of others. This is the kind of choice we all desire, the choice to act out of love, not out of obligation. It is good to give of yourself and help others, but *not at the expense of your own soul.* When you live with deliberate joy, you can give more fully of yourself when *you do choose to give.*

Pursue in life that which is most fitting to your nature. Pursue that which brings you joy and provides the atmosphere where you can be you. Imagine if you were pursuing the life choices you want—spiritual connectedness, good health, a career, a partner in life, your dream home. Your world would be a happier place.

I don't want to get to the end of my life
and find that I lived just the length of it.
I want to have lived the width of it as well.
~ Diane Ackerman

Spread Your Joy Deliberately

Have you ever noticed how you ask or are asked, "How are you?" when you encounter people? It is said in quick passing at the grocery store, around the coffeemaker at the office, when answering a telephone call.

The usual answer is "Fine." In fact, when you get a different response, don't you do a double take and pay attention? Let's take a look at this typical response.

When I hear someone respond to my "How are you?" with "Fine," what I really hear them saying is:

"My **F**eelings **I**nside are **N**o longer **E**nergized."

Or:

"I am **F**eeling **I**nternal **N**egative **E**nergy."

To respond with "I'm fine" says, "I don't want to go into details" . . . "Don't talk to me, I'm coasting right now" . . . "I'm being polite until I know what you really want" . . . "I'm surviving."

When asked "How are you?" do you respond with "I'm fine"? I challenge you to drop this from your list of autopilot responses. Instead, respond with words that will get people's attention because they reflect how joy-filled you really are. Elevate the asker with these alternative responses and you will often receive a smile. You'll feel better, too. This is one simple way to spread joy, and you may never know how beneficial the results can be, to you and to others.

Consider the words below and hear yourself using one of these responses when someone asks, "How are you?"

Happy	Elated	Excited
Energized	Joyful	Dandy
Grand	Fabulous	Fantastic
Wonderful	Terrific	Ecstatic
Splendid	Cheery	Lucky
Blessed	Life is grand.	Exhilarated

Add other words of your own.

____

____

____

____

Whenever I respond with one of these lively words, I get smiles in return. People do a double take, think for a moment, and then smile, laugh, or start up a conversation. Do not settle for being FINE. The word has lost its positive value as a response to the question of how you are. FINE is a word that cuts conversation short, stalls further questions, and withholds how you really feel. Joyful responses open a conversation in a positive way, or leave the asker feeling happy even if no conversation follows. Make someone smile by responding with your uplifting remark.

Benefits to Deliberate Joy

In Chapter Three, you read about the value to yourself of a smile. Now, see what a difference a smile can make to those around you. The simple act of smiling is a way to spread joy. Though you may not always feel the immediate effects of smiling and responding positively to others, there can be obvious rewards.

Have you ever found yourself smiling as you were shopping? I always get more attention if I am smiling, whether at a grocery store, a department store, or an office supply store. When you smile, you are more approachable.

Once, when I was flying home from a convention, the seats on the airline were oversold. Many disgruntled customers were standing in line complaining about the airline industry. My companions and I were near the line's end.

We were in our own world while we were waiting; what could we do anyway? We knew the situation was beyond our control. So there we stood, laughing and sharing stories from our recent convention. A ticket agent noticed us and walked past all those angry people straight to us, and asked us to step up to another counter. She told us we looked so joyful that she was going to give us the last four seats on the plane! She had had a tough day and the angry passengers were not helping her situation, so she chose us. Joy has its rewards!

Another time, I was headed to the airport and realized I was really late. I had pushed the time factor too far by doing everything I could on my checklist before leaving the house. I knew it was unlikely I would make my flight, but decided to keep going to the airport anyway. I figured once I was there, the ticket agent would book me on another flight, and I would get to my destination late. It was my own fault, so what more could I do? When I reached the ticket counter, it was twenty-five minutes before the flight was to leave. The agent said, "You're really pushing the envelope today, aren't you?" He was smiling and so was I, and I responded, "I figured you'd just put me on the next flight out since I'm this late." He chuckled, picked up his walkie-talkie and announced, "I've got one more coming up!" I was on my way. Even my luggage made it all the way to my destination. You never know when a smile and a joyful attitude will pay off in an immediate manner.

Determine in advance how you want to enter a situation. I knew when I was late for the airport it was my fault, and I would have to make the most of whatever opportunity presented itself. There could be no room for anger on my part toward anyone else. Determining this before I arrived at the airport enabled me to get what I wanted. Sometimes it works, and sometimes you have to live with the consequences of your actions. Be responsible for your own actions, your own behavior, and choose to be joyful despite less-than-desired situations.

If you know there is a tough topic to be handled at work and it is likely there will be a lot of negative emotions, decide before you go how you want to respond, so you are not caught up in the negative conversation. If going to a family event usually leaves you feeling exhausted and frustrated, decide in advance to go with the expectation that this is the way your family is, and you will not feed into any arguments. Give yourself the security and determination to remain in integrity with the joy you want. Disable others' ability to pop your bubble of joy with their negative energy. Rely on the strength of your joy to impact positively the situations you encounter.

Make the most of every situation with a smile on your face and joy in your heart. So often the situation everyone is complaining about is beyond one's control anyway. When others are having a tough day, your smile may make the difference. You will be someone to feel good about, which is how you start spreading joy to those around you who appear to be without it at the moment.

Joy is what happens to us when
we allow ourselves to recognize
how good things really are.
~ Marianne Williamson

7

Sustain Your Joy

Only when your consciousness is totally focused on the moment you're in can you receive whatever gift, lesson, or delight that moment has to offer.
~ Barbara De Angelis

You do not live alone. Your life is entangled and intertwined with the lives of many people around you: family, coworkers, friends, and neighbors. You're learning to live in your Joy Zone, but what if your spouse, your best friend, or a parent is definitely living without joy? Your most important relationships can either be a source of joy or a test of your Joy Zone. How does this affect you? How do you help or, more importantly, how do you cope? In this chapter you get to put joy into the context of daily living with others—everyday encounters with those to whom you are closest and chance encounters with people you meet along the way

We all experience joy differently and behave differently because of who we are and the influences in our lives. For whatever reason, some people choose to live in anger as a way of protecting themselves and controlling their emotions. Other people choose sarcasm as a way of protecting a sensitive nature and delicate ego. Sarcasm may be the way they grew up, so they don't know how to function any differently. Still others have functioned so long in despair, sadness, or crisis, that that is their norm.

Many people already live a very contented life, but they simply haven't thought about bringing it up a notch. They are content with what is comfortable. They don't realize they could tip the scale to an even higher level of joy.

Although you want to live with joy, it may not be what someone else desires—for themselves or for you! As you grow in joy, you will be forever in the company of people who are not growing and who may even resent the changes they see in you.

Timing is everything—for you and for others. Keep in mind that we all do the best we can in our individual circumstances until we learn something new and decide to change. We live the way we live until we have a reason or desire to live differently. You know yourself that no one knows when the time is right for you for change, growth, and joy, except you. Likewise, you don't know when the time is right for someone else; only they do. So let's explore your relationships with other people, keeping kindness and patience for ourselves and them in mind.

People change and forget
to tell each other.
~ Lillian Hellman

First, we'll discuss **Joy Stealers,** people who fuss over little things in life and miss out on the good things that come their way.

Next, we'll look at **Joy Suckers**, people who literally suck the joy right out of the room as soon as they enter. You know these people. Often they are the ones from whom you cannot get away, the permanent fixtures in your life.

Joy Distracters are people whose life circumstances have thrown them a curve ball. They are not joyless by nature, but they are going through a tough time. The way you sustain your joy is a huge benefit to them, but also a challenge to you as you try to maintain your own healthy perspective and stay in your Joy Zone.

Fortunately, there are plenty of **Joy Sparklers** around as well. They are the people who inspire us by who they are and how they live. The joy they live attracts an abundance of miracles. Gratitude is an unquestioned part of their lives. These are the people that uplift and expand your joy.

Finally, we will close this chapter by looking at ways to mend past relationships—with the living and non-living—so they can become a source of joy as well.

Joy Stealers

Likely you encounter these people most often. In the grocery store checkout aisle you may hear "Griping Gabby" fussing about the price of gas, the cost of milk, the hot weather, you name it. She spreads her gloom to whoever will listen and hopefully validate her cheerlessness by adding to the conversation. You may also know a "Debbie Downer," the office complainer who sits next to you and unloads her long list of complaints—the coffeemaker is broken in the staff lounge, someone parked in her parking space, and her secretary can't seem to do anything without being asked twice. Later in the day, "Negative Nellie" shows up at your health club, fuming about the facilities. She is never satisfied. If the club paints the women's locker room, she thinks they should have painted the outside of the building. If the club upgrades the treadmills, she thinks they should have added more weightlifting machines. You wish she would stop flexing her frowning muscles and exercise a few smiling muscles.

Joy Stealers are the people notorious for bursting other people's bubbles. If you announce you just bought a new car, they will tell you, "That's nice, but now you have to worry about it getting scratched, and I'll bet your insurance will go up, too." Or, "That's a great haircut, but I liked it better long." Their compliments are followed with a "but" which negates the compliment altogether.

The Joy Stealers' perspective will always be different from yours. To prevent them from stealing your joy, plan ahead:

1. Remember, no one can steal your joy without your permission.
2. Keep smiling and it will be more uncomfortable for Joy Stealers to unload their negative perspectives.
3. Acknowledge the Joy Stealers' comments, *and* acknowledge your feelings as well. Hold onto your joy no matter what.

With a Griping Gabby, you may need merely to smile and make a soft comment such as, "I don't mind a day of heat." Or you can flash an empathetic smile, turn away, and not even engage in conversation. When Debbie Downer starts in complaining at the next staff meeting, acknowledge her without telling her why she's wrong, and then redirect the conversation. For example: "Debbie, I can see why you feel that way, but since I'm not the one to fix it, I'm not spending my energy fussing about it." Then, ask her a question about something else to change the subject. "Did you see pictures of Catie Coworker's new puppy? Isn't it the cutest thing?" You'll shift her energy, and she'll begin to see that unloading her complaints on you will go nowhere.

Recognize that Joy Stealers are not out intentionally to ruin everyone else's day; they are simply looking for someone with whom to commiserate. Quite simply, they likely have not had a joy-filled day in a long time.

Who are the Negative Nellies, Griping Gabbys, and Downer Debbies in your life?

Pick one of the above, the one who invades your Joy Zone most often, and note what it is she says or does that steals your joy.

How will you keep your joy intact next time you encounter this person?

____

____

____

____

Have you heard the saying, "If you knew how much people were thinking about you, you would be disappointed"? That's because people in general are more focused on themselves, consciously or not. When it comes to Joy Stealers, keep in mind that what they say and do is all about them, not you. It is not their conscious intention to shake you out of joy, but rather more their way of controlling a situation.

There are times when a Joy Stealer sneaks in from out of the blue, an unknown in your life who makes a brief appearance. It could be a fender-bender on a busy day, a baby sitter who shows up late or not at all, someone who crosses your path while having a bad day or a moment of stupidity. When this happens, maintain your integrity by staying in your Joy Zone.

Here are two personal stories that show how I managed to stay focused on joy despite a couple of unexpected Joy Stealers in my life.

Story #1
Stolen Barbies

My mother, my daughter, and I had a one-day garage sale on an extremely hot, humid day. Typical of "professional rummagers," buyers arrived ready to shop an hour before we were ready to start. We started anyway and the rush of people was amazing. You'd have thought you were at a theme park when the gates were opening, to see these shoppers leap from their cars the moment our garage door opened. For an hour we had a mob of buyers. Mom and Karin were busy taking money, and I was frantically unloading boxes from the garage onto tables in the driveway.

After that first hour, we had a lull in shoppers for a short ten minutes. During those ten minutes, I was rearranging and refolding clothes at a table when I found a Barbie doll. I looked for the box full of Barbie dolls we had for sale, to put the stray doll with the others. We looked everywhere, but it was gone. Someone had walked off with a box of forty Barbie dolls, and we hadn't even seen it happen. We were dumbfounded. Who steals from a garage sale?!

We had a choice in how we would react. We were just starting the day. This thief could be a Joy Stealer, or we could let it go and move on. We chose to let it go. Everything left at the end of the day was to be donated anyway, so we would have given the dolls to them had they asked. The ones who stole the Barbies are the ones who have to live with their actions. We don't. We chose to maintain our Joy Zone for the day, have fun, and move on.

Story #2
A Lawsuit

One winter we had a lawsuit filed against us by a woman who had slipped on our icy sidewalk. Although the insurance adjusters, the attorney, and the insurance company all conceded it was a "no-fault" situation, the insurance company decided to pay her off rather than rack up more costs in attorney fees. Though angry at first, I had to use the **B.O.L.D.** approach, covered in Chapter Four, for two reasons: my own well-being, and because this woman lives in my community and I am likely to encounter her around town. I chose to discard the pain of frustration, trust the aid of Divine assistance, and believe there would be joy in the end. I was determined not to rant and rave or be angry about the situation. I was intent on being nice to this woman. I would not let her become a Joy Stealer in my life.

Many of our friends benefited from this situation, too, because it caused them to look at their own insurance policies and make some changes. Life situations are going to happen. When they do, you want to walk away from them with your joy still intact.

Joy Suckers

The toxic people in your life are Joy Suckers. Unfortunately, they can be family members, your best friend's rude husband (or your own), a coworker, maybe even your teenager or adult child. These are people you love, but it is a challenge to be in their presence.

Let's be real here. This person is not going to change overnight and is not going away. Your best friend is not getting a divorce, so her husband will be around awhile. You really do love your spouse; he's just irritating you at present. Your coworker is not going to be fired anytime soon. Your teenager may seem evil and have you thinking you are living in hell, or your adult child may be struggling to be independent while living under your roof, but they are still your children.

Since these situations are not going to dissolve overnight or in the foreseeable future, you need to decide how to stay in control of your emotions and maintain your Joy Zone. The trick is to find the positive in the person. Find the goodness in them. It may be a stretch, but you must shift your energy about these toxic people if you are to remain in your Joy Zone. Try this exercise.

Who are the most irritating Joy Suckers in your life right now? If you are afraid they will find this book and your notes, use a separate piece of paper or use initials. But do complete this exercise.

What are three good traits about each of the people you listed?

Wait, did you really write three? If not, think again, and write three good points for each Joy Sucker. You are doing this to be able to stay in your own Joy Zone. Learning to shift your focus from what irritates you to what energizes you will help you sustain your joy.

Now, take those three sentences and rewrite them in the first person. Put yourself in the sentence. Make it all about you for a minute.

For example, if you wrote, "She's a good cook" or "He takes good care of his lawn," change it to "I'm a good cook" or "I take good care of my lawn." If, on the other hand, you wrote a sentence with a touch of sarcasm, such as "At least she gets her hair colored" or "He has a hearty appetite," again, change those sentences to make them about you: "At least I get my hair colored" and "I have a hearty appetite." Now ask yourself, how positive do these sentences really sound? Does it feel uncomfortable to see them as a reflection of you? Is there any sarcasm in your sentences? The point is, do your best to find and celebrate some genuinely good traits about each of these people.

Everyone has potential for goodness and joy. Keep in mind that, deep down, you see in others what you see in yourself. Choose to focus on the good in others and that good will multiply. The essence of their negativity will dissolve or at least diminish because you no longer perceive that trait in the person as a dominant trait.

When you see someone differently, you treat him or her differently. In turn, you will be teaching them how to behave differently around you, too. You become an example of joy for them.

Another exercise to help you live with toxic people is to write out a list of *pros* to having them in your life. Then turn it around. What if this person were out of your life? We start thinking differently about people when we think what life would be like without them.

Examples of good things about these people in your life:

Family Member

My children have a grandparent to take them fishing.
She does have patience with our elderly parents.

Best Friend's Husband

She needs a stable man, and he's it.
He does love her and provides a lifestyle she likes.

Your Spouse or Partner

I haven't stopped loving him.
We have history together worth building on.
Our values are the same.

A Coworker

I can trust him to get his projects done for the firm.
She has a creative thought process we need here.

Teenager

My life would be lonely without this teen in my life.
He has a sense of humor.

Adult Child

She's such a great companion to her grandmother.
Her goofy impressions make me laugh.

List one major Joy Sucker, and the positives about that person in your life.

____

____

____

____

The longer you live in your Joy Zone, the less you will encounter the toxic side of others who do not live life from a perspective of joy or who habitually live life from the negative or sarcastic edge of life. When you spread joy by living it, you help shift people from a toxic approach to life to a joy-filled approach.

When someone else lives without joy, it is not because of you or about you. Living without joy is a choice they make for themselves. Your focus in this situation is how to maintain joy in the presence of Joy Suckers. Accept what is, as it is, and then move forward. Some things in life are not in your power to change. Your joy is in your power to maintain.

Ask for Divine assistance to arm you with a shield of joy before you approach toxic people. Remind yourself of your own talents. Review your gratitude journal. Take a time-out. Meditate or pray. Smile and elevate others. The toxic antics or attitudes of others will be repelled and you will walk away without scars.

You never know what makes someone toxic. You may think someone at work is negative because she is bitter she didn't get a promotion and you did when, in fact, her marriage or finances are in trouble. Your neighbor may be in a sour mood every time you walk your dogs and see him outside. How would you know he is terrified of dogs and your two gigantic canines, though friendly to all, scare the dickens out of him? You are not inside everyone else's head and heart to know why they act as they do. When you live in your Joy Zone, however, you are an example for others to follow and it is easier to function with others, too.

Though you impact your own life by the choices you make, there is a limit to what you can do to change another's life. They have to want to change. You change, but sometimes the people around you do not. If you are living with joy now and weren't when you started this book, it is because you made the choice to live differently. Spread your joy to all you encounter, starting with a simple smile.

Joy Distracters

Joy Distracters are people who normally live in the Joy Zone, but something happens to them. They are in a place and time in life where they hit a low spot, an unanticipated experience. Maybe they have lost a job, discovered they have cancer, or been blind-sided by an unexpected divorce. Maybe they have hit a personal, all-time low and rekindled an addiction to gambling, alcohol, or prescription medications.

When someone in your life experiences a death, a crisis, an injustice, or trauma, where do you fit in? How do you sustain joy when those around you cannot? You know they did live in joy and will again, although now may be a time when they need to live through other emotions first.

Divorce is a major Joy Distracter for many women. As you witness friends or family members go through divorce, make sure you support them, empathize, and pray with them. Do not, however, get caught up in the emotions they are experiencing, let alone relive your own negative emotions if you, too, are divorced. The joy distraction is theirs, not yours.

It isn't always easy, especially when someone so close has been horribly treated, betrayed, or abandoned for someone or something else. Put your energy into being a positive diversion for them. When you sustain your joy, you bring hope to those who are experiencing tough times.

Call on your best Joy Builders, tune into your Joy Receptors, and keep living your own life in the Joy Zone.

Friends of ours had a child who was charged with an unimaginable crime. They found their lives turned upside down. Every member of their family was stressed and uncertain of the outcome. They were torn and hurting. They began to blame others and wish not for justice, but for revenge. Their fun-loving, easygoing life had been ripped apart by the incident. Many people in their friendship circle came to their aid. At the time of this joy distraction, a joy-filled life seemed too much even to dream about.

When we spent time with them, my husband and I realized we had to vent our feelings of frustration about the whole situation to each other, but then, before spending time with our kids or anyone else again, we needed to release our feelings and be open to experiencing joy.

When you give of yourself to aid others in pain, perhaps by listening to their troubles or helping them out with deeds, it is important to leave the pain of their situation behind when you depart their presence.

Make a conscious choice to let go of their problems and clear your mind. Ask for Divine assistance for them, and for the negative energies to be removed from you so you can refocus on what is good. There is no benefit to suffering on another's behalf—sometimes easier said than done. It is good to help others, but not to suffer on their behalf. Suffering is optional. Staying in your own Joy Zone is, too.

Joy is the net of love by which
you can catch souls.
~ Mother Teresa

Joy Sparklers

Joy Sparklers are the people you love to be around. They are the ones who have great energy in life; they exude happiness. Their joy is deep in their souls and gratitude is a way of life. You are always comfortable in their presence. They seek to be of service to others. They may be the ones who make you laugh or calm your nerves. And, when Joy Sparklers are faced with their own challenges, their gratitude still shines. A circumstance in life may shake up their daily routine, but the essence of who they are remains unchanged. Hope and joy are a part of their life. They inspire you to live with deliberate joy.

Joy Sparkler Stories

Story #1

My dear friend Lisa is an absolute Joy Sparkler. Lisa loves life, loves kids, and would do anything for a friend in need. She makes me laugh, she creates fun wherever she goes, and she warms my heart with her accepting personality.

I had a busy afternoon planned including an outing with my Grandma to my kids' school music program and then a business seminar. I took Grandma to hear the kids sing, expecting the program to last forty-five minutes. After the program, I expected to have enough time to take Grandma home, then head out to the airport to pick up a company executive. The program started late and, as it was passing the hour mark, I was getting worried. I didn't want to take Grandma home before it was over. I didn't want to miss my kids singing. I didn't want Grandma to have to run out to the airport with me and then around town until I could get her back home. Who would I put in the back seat—Grandma or the executive? And I couldn't leave a company executive standing curbside at the airport. I had not made provisions in my schedule for extra time, anywhere.

I ended up asking Lisa, who had just met Grandma, if she could drive her home after the program. Lisa not only took Grandma home, she spent the rest of the afternoon with her, driving her around town, listening to all her stories, and stopping by her own house to pick up a freshly baked loaf of banana bread for Grandma to take home with her. Lisa often and lovingly retells the story of spending time with my Grandma. Grandma loved her time with Lisa and her kids, and she really appreciated the banana bread, too. Lisa pops in and rescues me when I overload and need her. I am blessed to have her in my life.

Lisa spreads joy to others by her compassion for their needs. She frequently takes an elderly person out grocery shopping or looks after a family who is down-and-out. I was happy to have the opportunity to help her with a family down on their luck, giving her clothes for their children. Lisa was delighted and delivered the clothes right away. Then she made a donation to a local charity in my name in appreciation for my help. Lisa is a woman of joy, and she spreads it to others.

Story #2

Death nearly claimed the life of Mike and Jan Naborowski's daughter, Tia. At the tender age of seven, her organs suddenly shut down without explanation and she went into cardiac arrest three times in seven days. The impact on her body was decreased oxygen to the brain, causing brain damage. Tia was in the intensive care unit for forty days. Neither the attending physicians nor the specialists could determine the cause of her rapidly declining health. The doctors suspected Tia had a rare genetic disease that would cause her to die within the year. They also said her two sisters had a 50 percent chance of experiencing the same disorder and they too would die young. The following twelve months flooded our friends' lives with Tia's therapy, bills, questions, and heartache, and yet they believed through it all that their child would walk, talk, and function again.

The final diagnosis was encephalitis caused by the West Nile virus. This came as some relief to the Naborowski family, both to have a diagnosis and realize that genetics were not involved. Two years later, Tia has regained her ability to live, walk, and learn. Mike and Jan envisioned over and over during her hospital stay that Tia would one day run and play with others again and even walk down the aisle in her own wedding. They prayed that their family life would return to normal. They looked for, expected, and found miracles and were grateful for the help, assistance, and worldwide prayers sent their way. They found joy in and around the anger, fear, and sadness of their child's situation.

The Naborowski family's challenges are still not over. Therapy will continue for six days a week as Tia continues to improve her strength, balance, and ability to walk. One day, she will take a victory lap around the soccer field, holding her leg braces high in the air. Her smile will reflect the joy of victory. Jan and Mike's tears will reflect the joy in their hearts. Until that day, Jan and Mike recognize each little improvement as a milestone to be joyful about and celebrate.

All of us have the same opportunity to view any given situation in any manner we choose. Though our friends experienced moments of desperation, anger, fear, sadness, and even helplessness, they continue to choose to keep moving forward with gratitude and joy.

When have you witnessed another person or family experiencing tragedy, challenges, or trauma that left you amazed at the positive position they adopted throughout the ordeal?

____

____

____

____

Only when we are no longer afraid
do we begin to live.
~ Dorothy Thompson

Story #3

In the summer of 2004, our close friend Gary Rhone was diagnosed with Creutzfeldt-Jakob Disease (CJD), a very rare disease that, in layperson's terms, is much like the human version of mad cow disease. His brain malfunction came on quickly, and in less than three months he went from a robust, fun-loving, intelligent man to one who couldn't walk or talk, and was sinking fast. In just four-and-a-half months, he was gone.

Gary was young, only 57 years old, with five small grandchildren and a great wife whom we love and adore. My children loved Gary like a grandfather. As I shed tears, I have this deep feeling of gratitude that Gary has been a part of our lives. I am thankful that he had a positive relationship with his children. I have always admired his love for his wife, Joyce. Everyone who knew Gary experienced sadness, helplessness, and disbelief, throughout his illness and his death.

To watch the Rhone family was a reminder to rise above our own life issues and live with deliberate joy. Even in his declining physical state, Gary still continued to impact others positively. I witnessed his son, Jeff, in a complete role reversal, caring for his father's needs with love and compassion. His daughter, Lisa, ran the household when Joyce could not.

Gary brought out the best in everyone. I watched my husband compassionately step in and assist in decisions for Gary, and for the health and well-being of the entire family. Nurses and aides at the nursing home gave loving care and took time to learn about CJD so they could best serve Gary. Joyce and Gary's family members all helped out at their home. I observed my own son, at the age of five, be a compassionate soul toward Gary and Joyce. He drew pictures for Gary's hospital room and went with me to visit Gary in the nursing home.

The Rhones took advantage of their last months together, taking Gary horseback riding, connecting with family, taking lots of photos, and spending time together. Many people stepped in with support, food, prayers, time for silence, and hugs for Joyce and her children. During those four-and-a-half months there was joy as we reminisced about all our fun times and "remember whens." Today we still celebrate Gary and keep his memory alive.

Have you experienced a personal loss, or maybe even several, through the death of loved ones? Maybe you've lost a mother, your spouse, a child, or a best friend. Are you at a point where you can find joy in the relationship you had, joy because you had time together, joy because your life was enriched by this person's presence? Eternal sorrow on your part does not honor your loved one who is no longer physically present. Revitalize yourself by focusing on those good experiences.

List the joys of the relationship you had with a loved one— happy memories you cherish.

____

____

____

____

You may want to transfer these happy memories to your memory book so they are at hand when you want or need to remember.

Don't ruin the present
with the ruined past.
~ Ellen Gilchrist

Mending the Past

Do you have a pain in your heart for someone who was hard to deal with, but now that they are gone, you miss them and the opportunity to make things better? You may be left with a feeling of emptiness or discontent. There may always be an uncomfortable void when the family gathers and shares stories, and you are unable to experience any memories of joy. Instead, you experience uneasiness, frustration, or even anger.

If there is someone who has passed on with whom you didn't have a good relationship and about which you now have regrets, you *can* go back and mend that relationship. Odd as it may sound, it is possible. And, you'll feel better for it.

Write out a list of positives about this person as you did earlier about the Joy Suckers in your life. Now focus on the positives regarding this person. It may feel strange or uncomfortable at first, but start writing anyway.

Next, visualize yourself having a conversation with this person. Write a letter and pour out every negative emotion you have, and then ask to be released of your poor relationship and from any guilt you harbor. In your letter, state you are ready for a positive, happy relationship. Does this sound crazy to you? It did to me. When I tried it, though, I immediately understood the healing power of this exercise.

What are some points you want to be sure to write about more thoroughly in your letter to this person?

In writing this letter you are, in a way, rewriting your history with that person. You are continuing a conversation you both would have wanted to have. You are taking advantage of the chance to create good memories by revisiting the past and bringing a new perspective to it. You can now look back at that relationship with a sense of calm and better memories because you know you have done all you can to mend that relationship.

Think of a sign that will be a symbol or reminder of the good times with that person. Anytime I see an American flag or hear a patriotic song, I think of my Grandpa Roland. He was very patriotic as a veteran, which I admired, but his prejudiced beliefs I detested. I choose now to focus on the good things in life that he did, and see him as a loving guardian in heaven. When my son belts out the song "God Bless the USA" by Lee Greenwood, I picture Grandpa right there smiling with immense pride. When I see old photos of Grandpa holding my children as babies, I see him in heaven holding the miscarried babies we've never been able to hold ourselves.

Grandpa Roland and my Grandma Esther were quite a pair. They were my grandparents and I loved them, but they could sure push joy out when they got started talking about their strong religious or political beliefs. There was never much room for a differing opinion.

As a kid, I did not like my Grandmother Esther very much. She was cross, negative, and pessimistic. She seemed so out of touch with my generation. I did not like the way she treated my mother either. Still, when Grandma was in her last months of cancer, my mother made her homemade soups, and sewed shawls and cover-ups that would keep her warm but not interfere with all the tubes she had in her. I struggled with this for a long time.

Just before Grandmother Esther died, several of her children and their spouses were standing around her bedside talking. While they were visiting with each other, my mother shared a private moment with Grandma. Although Grandma could barely speak, her nod and the look in her eyes was an acknowledgment to Mom that everything was okay. In that moment of acknowledgment, their relationship was mended. Mine took a bit longer.

In looking back, I've come to better understand that my grandmother used her pessimism to protect herself. She was not a woman of great confidence, yet in tough economic times she raised five children. She was active in her church, was a woman of deep faith, and she could out-knit anyone. Now, when my children are a complete challenge to me, I picture Grandma saying, "I survived raising kids, and you will, too." I feel her presence in our hours of need and now experience my own loving and mended relationship with Grandma.

Spirit is the real and eternal;
matter is the unreal and temporal.
~ Mary Baker Eddy

Visualizing a positive situation or writing a letter can be a good exercise to move you through some not-so-good emotions. There can be great comfort in creating a positive relationship with someone who has passed on, now that they are gone. In time, you will find the joy coming back. If you have not yet found the joy after the death of a loved one, it would be wise to seek out a counselor, learn about the stages of grief, and then—and I say this with the utmost compassion and care—get on with life.

Trust the process of life.

Everyone is living life as they believe they should be. Aren't you? Really, aren't you living the best life you can right now? Living the best life you can live right now may mean you are in the midst of self-discovery, of redefining who you are, who you want to be, and how you want to exist in your world. You cannot look at another person and determine they should live differently. It's quite possible the way they are living now is 100 percent better then the way they were living a year ago. One person's anger may be a step above living in depression. One person's frustrations may be one step above living in constant anger. One person's casual demeanor may be one step above living in constant worry.

The task for you when faced with someone who is angry, frustrating, or an endless naysayer, is to stay in your own Joy Zone. You don't have to join in the negative emotions of others. You can listen, offer advice if asked, and then simply walk away. You, living in your Joy Zone, will be the guidepost for someone who seeks joy in her life and is on her way to getting there. It is likely you didn't arrive in your Joy Zone in a day or a week, but only through continuous growth, introspection, and through other joy-filled people in your life—the Joy Sparklers. In every endeavor, you are a witness to someone around you. If you focus on living in your Joy Zone, others will see it and find themselves changing without knowing why.

Patience. Peace. Acceptance. When you practice these virtues, you will continue to sustain your own Joy Zone and transfer joy to those around you.

8

Last Words
Generate Your Joy

Stretch out your hand and take the world's wide gift of Joy and Beauty.
~ Corinne Roosevelt Robinson

Joy is something you create because you desire a life of exuberance, goodness, exhilaration, dreams, and abundance. It makes you want to dance, smile, and sing. It is the way you love yourself. Your Joy Zone is the place you get to, when you are fully connected to who you are right now—not who you think you could be or should be, or who others expect you to be. Your Joy Zone is where you accept yourself completely for who you are and what makes you happy—your own personal celebration of life and all its opportunities. It is a place of peace, tranquility, acceptance, and deep-breathing comfort, all rising from within the depth of your own being.

What are you waiting for? Your Inner Being, God, the Universe, whatever entity you believe to be at your center, is waiting for you! Like the woman walking the halls of heaven with St. Peter, gifts are surrounding you, all waiting to be unwrapped by your eyes, your heart, and your soul.

You can find joy in everything through the simple act of gratitude. You just have to see it. Every time you do, you'll be a light in the lives of the people around you. You begin to impact others without even knowing it, simply because they witness your personal joy. Your joy does make a difference to others.

Flying home from a family trip to San Diego with our kids and my mother, I experienced an overwhelming feeling of, "*If it were all over today, I could go in peace, without regret, feeling good about all that I am.*" Mind you, I have no intention of leaving this world anytime soon, but the feeling of total peace in my soul is joy at its highest level. And isn't this what we all want for ourselves and each other?

Recently, my eleven-year-old daughter Ellie and I were talking about faith, and our friends and family members who have passed on. She shared with me that she often feels their presence in her life and, when it's time, she will be ready to go to heaven. She told me she's not ready to leave right now, but when the time comes, she will not be afraid to die. It was a moment in my parenting when I was reminded how much the way we live influences others, especially those who are watching us most closely. Through her sharing some rather deep ideas and feelings for a child, Ellie truly exposed her inner joy with where she is in life, and I was privileged to hear it all.

My hope for you is that you will find that inner peace in your heart. My hope for you is that you are on a path to understanding how you want to feel joy, how to shift when you don't feel it, and how to generate more of it.

I encourage you to talk to yourself and continually ask, "Am I acting in a manner that will manifest joy in my life, or am I holding back for some reason?" When you are holding back from joy, remember that you can make a quick mental shift back to your Joy Zone. When you are in a state of creating and experiencing joy, be aware of how you got there, and then keep finding new ways to bring that joy into other parts of your life.

Your life is what it is because of the choices you have made so far. As you already know, these choices will take you to either the pits or the possibilities in life. You have the power to make choices and changes that will give you the life you are intended to live—a life filled with joy. Everyone deserves joy in life. YOU deserve joy in life. Start today.

When you can see what makes you happy and love what makes you real, that, my friend, is when you *Find Your Joy Zone.*

From this moment onward you can be an entirely different person,
filled with love and understanding, ready with an outstretched hand,
uplifted and positive in every thought and deed.
~ Eileen Caddy

101 Joy-Building Activities

Attend a play
Bake cookies
Bake cupcakes for your neighbors
Build a bonfire
Build a sandcastle
Build a snowman
Buy a magazine
Call an old friend
Clean out a drawer or closet
Compliment someone
Cross-stitch
Daydream
Do yoga
Donate to a charity
Draw a funny picture
Dress up
Drive a go-cart
Learn to fly
Learn something new
Learn to inline skate
Light a candle
Listen to music
Listen to someone else play the piano
Look through old photo albums
Frame a child's work of art

Get a body wrap
Get a massage
Get a facial
Get a new haircut
Get a pedicure
Go bird watching
Go camping
Go skiing
Go to an art gallery
Go to a movie
Go for a hike
Go to a museum
Go swimming
Go dancing
Go to a park with a picnic lunch just for you
Golf
Host a party
Ice skate
Invite someone to dinner
Knit
Learn a new language
Listen to a comedian
Make pancakes for dinner
Nap in the shade
Needlepoint
Paint a picture
Paint a room in your home
Paint your nails
Pet your cat or dog
Pick fresh flowers for your home and give some to a friend
Plant a garden
Play a board game
Play a card game with kids
Play tea party with a child
Play tennis
Play the piano

Play with toys
Quilt
Read a humorous book
Rearrange your living room or bedroom
Rearrange your artwork
Relax in a hot tub
Rent a classic movie
Ride a bike
Ride a horse
Roast marshmallows
Rock a baby
Run
Scrapbook
Send a funny card to a friend
Sew
Sing
Smile
Soak in a bubble bath
Swim
Take a Sunday drive in the countryside
Tour a historical building
Tour your city
Trim the trees
Update your wardrobe
Use the good china
Vacation
Visit a good friend
Visit the zoo
Visit www.YourJoyZone.com
Volunteer at a soup kitchen
Walk the dog
Watch a sunset
Watch home movies
Wear jewelry
Wear perfume
Work with clay

Write down memories of your favorite times with family
Write out your dreams
Write a love letter to a family member
Write a book!

This is just the beginning—

Write to me and share your joy-building activities—you may find them featured on our Web site, www.YourJoyZone.com.

Reading Suggestions & Resources for Your Joy Development

Allen, James. *As You Think*. Novato, CA: New World Library, 1998.

Andrews, Andy. *The Traveler's Gift*. Nashville, TN: Thomas Nelson Publishers, 2002.

Canfield, Jack, Mark Victor Hansen, and Les Hewitt. *The Power of Focus*. Deerfield Beach, FL: Health Communications, Inc., 2000.

Doheny, Kathleen. "Lighten Up: A Chuckle A Day." *WebMD Feature Archives.* http://my.webmd.com/content/Article/14/1668_50995.htm.

Dyer, Wayne W. *Manifest Your Destiny*. New York: HarperCollins Publishers, HarperPerennial, 1997.

———. *The Power of Intention*. Carlsbad, CA: Hay House, Inc., 2004.

Ellis, Albert. *How to Stubbornly Refuse to Make Yourself Miserable about Anything—Yes, Anything!* New York: Kensington Publishing Corp., Lyle Stuart, 1988.

Ellis, Albert, and Irving Becker. *A Guide to Personal Happiness*. Hollywood, CA: Wilshire Book Co., 1982.

Glasser, William, M.D. *Choice Theory*. New York: HarperCollins Publishers, HarperPerennial, 1998.

Grabhorn, Lynn. *Excuse Me, Your Life Is Waiting*. Charlottesville, VA: Hampton Roads Publishing Co., 2000.

Healthwise, Incorporated. "Humor Therapy: Topic Overview." *WebMD Medical Reference from Healthwise.* http://my.webmd.com/hw/alternative_medicine/tp21261.asp?printing=true.

Hicks, Esther, and Jerry Hicks. *Ask and It Is Given.* Carlsbad, CA: Hay House Inc., 2004.

McGraw, Phillip C. *Life Strategies: Doing What Works, Doing What Matters.* New York: Hyperion, 1999.

———. *Self Matters: Creating Your Life from the Inside Out.* New York: Simon & Schuster, Simon & Schuster Source, 2001.

Maxwell, John C. *The Success Journey.* Nashville: Thomas Nelson Publishers, 1997.

———. *Thinking for a Change.* New York: Warner Books, Inc., 2003.

National Sleep Foundation. "2005 Sleep in America Poll: Summary of Findings." http://www.sleepfoundation.org/_content/hottopics/2005_summary_of_findings.pdf.

Orman, Suze. *The Courage to Be Rich.* New York: Penguin Putnam Inc., Riverhead Books, 1999.

Osgood, Charles. "Gratitude Theory: Researchers Find the Virtues of Gratitude Include Good Health." *ACFnewsource.* http://www.acfnewsource.org/religion/gratitude_theory.html.

Osterweil, Neil. "He Who Laughs, Lasts." *WebMD Medical News Archives.* http://my.webmd.com/content/article/36/1728_64481.htm.

Pearson, Pat. *You Deserve the Best: How to Stop Self Sabotage And Deserve More.* Dallas, TX: Connemara Press, 1991.

Richardson, Cheryl. *Life Makeovers.* New York: Random House, Inc., Broadway Books, 2000.

Rohn, Jim. *The Five Major Pieces to the Life Puzzle: A Guide to Personal Success.* Southlake, TX: Dickinson Press, 1991.

———. *The Seasons of Life.* Irving, TX: Jim Rohn International, 1981.

Ross, Ruth. *Prosperity: A Woman's Guide.* New York: MJF Books, 1995.

Ruiz, Don Miguel. *The Four Agreements*. San Rafael, CA: Amber-Allen Publishing, Inc., 1997.

Schlitz, Marilyn, and Tina Amorok, with Marc S. Micozzi. *Consciousness & Healing: Integral Approaches to Mind-Body Medicine.* St. Louis, MO: Elsevier Churchill Livingstone, 2005.

Van Meter, Roz, and Pat Pearson. *Passion! Rekindling the Fire in Your Heart.* Dallas, TX: Hollingsworth Press, 1994.

Virtue, Doreen. *Healing With The Angels: How the Angels Can Assist You in Every Area of Your Life.* Carlsbad, CA: Hay House, Inc., 1999.

About the Author

Anne Nelson—author, speaker, and direct-sales entrepreneur—has studied her own and other women's lives both to tackle what's missing and openly celebrate what makes us thrive. Often sought out by others because of her "old soul" wisdom, she knows one must discover how to create joy now in order to experience it on the front end of life, not just the back end. Her young spirit inspires others to start living their lives with joy. She's a popular speaker among groups of businesswomen of all ages and all levels of success.

Whether it's keeping up with three children, supporting her husband in his work, volunteering, or assisting women in their businesses, Anne walks her talk. For more information about having Anne speak to your organization, visit her on the web at www.YourJoyZone.com.

A Personal Invitation

Additional *Your Joy Zone* books are in the works—please join us! I invite you to share your stories, experiences, and insights about these specific areas of your life—parenting, relationships, and working from home. Describe your challenges, your joy-filled moments, what makes you want to give up, and what keeps you going. Or, simply submit your questions. We're looking forward to hearing from you!

Please email your comments to:
Anne Nelson
info@YourJoyZone

Or send your comments to Anne at:
Your Joy Zone
5005 S. Jasmine Trail
Sioux Falls, SD 57108